TWENTIETH CENTURY INTERPRETATIONS
OF

HENRY IV
PART ONE

TWENTIETH CENTURY INTERPRETATIONS
OF

HENRY IV

PART ONE

A Collection of Critical Essays
Edited by
R. J. DORIUS

Prentice-Hall, Inc. *Englewood Cliffs, N. J.*

Copyright © 1970 by Prentice-Hall, Inc., Englewood Cliffs, New Jersey. A SPEC-
TRUM BOOK. All rights reserved. No part of this book may be reproduced in
any form or by any means without permission in writing from the publisher.
C–13-387043-X; P–13-387035-9. *Library of Congress Catalog Card Number 72–
126812.* Printed in the United States of America.

Current printing (last number):
10 9 8 7 6 5 4 3 2 1

PRENTICE-HALL INTERNATIONAL, INC. (*London*)
PRENTICE-HALL OF AUSTRALIA, PTY. LTD. (*Sydney*)
PRENTICE-HALL OF CANADA, LTD. (*Toronto*)
PRENTICE-HALL OF INDIA PRIVATE LIMITED (*New Delhi*)
PRENTICE-HALL OF JAPAN, INC. (*Tokyo*)

For C. P. D.

Contents

TWENTIETH CENTURY INTERPRETATIONS
OF

HENRY IV
PART ONE

Introduction

by R. J. Dorius

The ambiguity of the roles of Prince Hal and Falstaff has generated one of the liveliest sustained debates in all Shakespearean studies. Throughout this controversy, Hal's relationship to time is viewed as paramount, for it determines his relationship to himself, to other men, to heroism, and to government or power. In *Henry IV, Part One*, as private man in Eastcheap, Hal steps out of the public time associated with his father, at least in part so that he can learn to know himself and other types of men. But as prince, in soliloquy and at court, Hal promises to redeem the time so spent by locking himself into history and into an acknowledged association with heroism and kingship. Because of Hal's double nature, both the free spending and the husbanding of time are necessary, and yet they are at once mutually exclusive and complementary. When most a truant to chivalry, Hal is mindful of his future role as king. In *Part Two,* the paradoxes of *Part One* are sharpened, for here Hal, after heroic action, is again profaning the time with his private friends and yet moving in terms of public life between Shrewsbury and Westminster.

Hal's growing alliance with time is partly defined by Hotspur's gambling with it and Falstaff's ignoring it. In *Part One* Falstaff suspends time, amusing his friends and heightening their sense of life. But he is incapable of relating to the larger world which Hal must inhabit and control. At Gadshill Falstaff robs the King's exchequer, and at Shrewsbury he carries sack instead of a pistol on the battlefield. In *Part Two* he ignores the King's Justice, misuses the King's press for the second time, and boasts ominously and extravagantly about his role when Hal becomes king. Furthermore, in *Part Two* Falstaff amuses his friends less and begins to use or mislead them more. If Hal's movement from man and prince to king is towards the weighing of time, Falstaff's from companion to "vanity" is towards greater abuses of time. Both men are opportunists—Hal chiefly for the realm and Falstaff for himself—and the plays do not ignore the disturbing resonances set up between these spheres. Yet clearly the prince will reject the knight when Falstaff's private ethics threaten Hal's newly acquired public values. The problem of Hal's doubleness can be approached in various ways with varying conclusions—in terms of *Henry IV, Part One* itself, of the four plays in the Lancastrian cycle, of dominant patterns in Shakespearean tragedy and comedy, and of Shakespeare's changing attitudes between the 1590s and 1600s towards the roles of power and love in human life.

I

As we can see in the volumes on the histories in this series, commentators upon Prince Hal and Falstaff frequently tend to emphasize either the public good or the private—either the maintenance of strong government and therefore qualities like duty and responsibility, or the full development of the self and the capacity to be fully alive in the present. Hal's friends often differentiate sharply between the policy of the king and the honor and chivalry of his son. They point to Hal's growth in the military and civil virtues rather than to the ambiguities of his first soliloquy in *Part One* or of his rejection of Falstaff in *Part Two*. Falstaff's friends often see Hal as the somewhat cold-blooded son of a Lancaster who knows too much about making offense a skill. They emphasize the price of the Prince's exchange in *Part Two* of the friendship of Falstaff for the kingship. Today, more than ever before, interpretations of the play tend to fall on one side or the other of the pleasure principle. In an age which often sees arguments for power or military glory as hypocritical or corrupt, many readers are inclined to be Falstaffian, to see all of Bolingbroke's ways (and therefore Hal's) as indirect and crooked, and to see Hotspur and even Hal from Falstaff's point of view, as being absurd in the role of mailèd Mars. A considered reading, however, must balance the claims of Hal as hero against those of Falstaff as clown. Two of our difficulties with *Henry IV* can be stated simply: Hal is one of the few protagonists in Shakespeare outside of the comedies who succeeds without much suffering. With the tragedies in mind, we find it hard to forgive him for this good fortune, or to forgive similar well-meaning if manipulative figures (like the Duke in *Measure for Measure*) for being more plotters than plotted, subjects rather than objects of fate. But Hal is not only spared bad luck; in *Part Two* he banishes with impunity his tutor and friend, perhaps disavowing a part of his own nature.

Clearly, to accept Hal we must understand the particular virtues and limitations of the history play.

Shakespeare's tragedies often exhibit a pattern whereby the heroic figure, egged on by a tempter of sorts, challenges or kills a power figure or someone dear to the hero. We think of Cassius' goading Brutus to challenge Caesar and of other combinations—the Ghost, Hamlet, and Claudius; Iago, Othello, and Desdemona; the witches and Lady Macbeth, Macbeth, and Duncan; and Cleopatra, Antony, and Caesar. The hero is torn between two forces which can be seen at once as instruments of fate and aspects of himself. He becomes the battleground for warring powers or values in society and the universe. And, we might say, one side of his nature destroys the other as his little kingdom of man suffers the nature of an insurrection. Now Hal is tempted by his father ruffian, Falstaff, to scorn old father antic the law in the person of his real father, Henry IV. But, unlike the heroes of tragedy, Hal is permitted to enlarge his powers rather than go to buffets with himself, to incorporate rather than destroy the virtues of both fathers. In *Henry IV, Part One* he is therefore not called upon to kill the King; he merely absents himself most of the time from the King and his mistreadings, and at Shrewsbury he even saves the King's life. It is Hotspur instead who poses the principal challenge to Henry IV in absolutist terms that remind us of the tragic heroes. But Harry of Monmouth kills the rebel Harry instead of the royal Henry, and he assimilates Hotspur's virtues as he does those of other men. We are prevented from responding in tragic terms to this killing partly because Falstaff parodies it, in a scene which is one of the most daring of Shakespeare's juxtapositions of heroic and comic. Falstaff rises from the dead as the hero never can, rejoicing in the "better part of valor" and mocking grinning honor. The tragic formula is clearly crossed in *Henry IV, Part One* with a comic pattern.

In the romantic comedies, the principal characters go through a series of trials in which heart and head discipline and test each other and as a result of this interplay the protagonists emerge united and happy. Hal too goes through a series of trials which often take, as in comedy, the form of wit-combats and plays within plays, and he also emerges triumphant. The disguise of contagious clouds, like the male disguise of the heroines of comedy, enables Hal to try on roles and to widen his experience of life. The pattern of *Henry IV, Part One* and especially the pattern of *Henry V,* in which Hal conquers France and woos its princess, are thus variations upon a basic comic rhythm. But the second time Shakespeare tells Hal's story, in *Henry IV, Part Two,* he tilts it further toward tragedy. Here ⌊Hal banishes one of his fathers when the other (conveniently) dies.⌋ Again he is spared the actual killing of the tragedies. And the father he banishes is the tempter-figure who in the tragedies commits the hero to self-division and therefore self-destruction.⌋

⌊*Henry IV, Part One* is therefore poised between tragedy and comedy, and yet its values are different from those of both.⌋ In tragedy, time must have a stop, as it does for Hotspur, because the hero is on a collision course with himself and the cosmos. He has no second chance, and release and ultimate value can only be acquired through self-transcendence in death. In the first act of Shakespearean comedy, time also seems stopped by a threat to the lovers, but then they are given a reprieve in both time and space, as Hal is with Falstaff in Eastcheap. The lovers in comedy, while discovering and liberating themselves in garden or forest, and before returning to the court, are, as Frye says, outside time, in the green world. The values explored and asserted by characters in comedy or tragedy, achieved as they are partly through the garden, the dream, or death, are only partly those associated, as in *Henry IV*, with a prince's education for kingship. Eastcheap is in a sense Hal's garden, where his witty and affectionate companionship with Falstaff prepares him to return with deeper humanity to the life at court. But only in *Henry IV* among the histories is the timeless world richly life-enhancing and fully developed as a commentary upon struggles for power. The garden in most of the histories, unlike that of the comedies, is overgrown with weeds, an emblem of the paralysis or sickness of the state. Even in *Henry IV, Part One* the May games and other rites of comedy have become a robbery at Gadshill, the vine has become sack, the clown is fat and corrupt, and the Prince, having no time or disposition for love, is always aware that he is idling and profaning the precious time. After the middle of the play, the Prince confronts neither the escape hatches of comedy nor the finality of tragedy. Time is here a medium which Hal, the only leader whose luck matches his gifts, can exploit, in which he can plod like a man for working days, for achievement. Hal is not asked, as the tragic heroes are, to explore the limits of human nature but to become a well-rounded man of action. And because Falstaff has nothing to do with the time of the day, because he does not know when jesting and dallying are inappropriate or dangerous, he will not even be hangman in the new reign.

Hal's relationship to time in *Henry IV, Part One* is developed in two major movements. In the first two acts, Hal primarily learns the language of timelessness in Eastcheap. In his soliloquy (I.ii.218), he drops his disguise to tell the audience that he will a while uphold the unyoked humor of his friends' idleness but that he will finally please again to be himself, redeeming time. In the play-acting scene, the man of all humors promises ("I do, I will") to banish Falstaff (II.iv.528). Thus freed from the inner rebellion which led him to the tavern, Hal is ready to turn to the outer rebellion of the Percys against his father. He now steps into history and the road to Shrewsbury. He moves in the last three acts from the promise he gives his father (III.ii) to redeem the time in the closing of some glorious day, to that day itself, when he rescues the father he had seemed to hate (V.iv), hears Henry pronounce the releasing formula —"Thou hast redeem'd thy lost opinion"—and conquers the rebel Hotspur in single fight.

Even in the histories, as we have seen, only Hal is able to ride happily in tandem with destiny. The Prince begins his career with the dainty ear which Richard II confesses he only developed at the end of his life:

> here have I the daintiness of ear
> To check time broke in a disordered string,
> But for the concord of my state and time
> Had not an ear to hear my true time broke.
> I wasted time, and now doth time waste me. (V.v.45)

Richard had of course destroyed this concord by committing crimes which, as York warned him, stopped the stream of time. Henry IV, who rationalizes in *Part Two* that "necessity so bow'd the state/ That I and greatness were compell'd to kiss" (III.i.73), confesses before he dies that his usurpation reduced his time to an obsessive and defensive moment: "For all my reign hath been but as a scene/ Acting that argument." Hal alone, freed from obsession, learns as king how to weigh time "Even to the utmost grain." He is lucky. He is throughout far more "sweet Fortune's minion and her pride" than Hotspur, who heedlessly attempts to force events and thus renders his life time's fool. Hal combines something of the wise passiveness of Hamlet's "The readiness is all" with the freely operating intelligence of the heroines of comedy. And though both Hal and Hamlet are haunted by the murder of a king which has thrown time out of joint, Hamlet is committed to set it right by avenging his uncle's murder of his own father, whereas Hal, prodded by no ghost, need only *atone* (in *Henry V*) for his father's murder of Richard II, an act which is less central to his imagination. Hal is given the time, like Hamlet, to discriminate among rival selves— the man the King wishes the Prince to be (Harry Hotspur), the man the Prince seems to be ("engrafted" to Falstaff), the man he really is (a late bloomer), and the man he will become (advised by the Chief Justice; self-directing). And Hal, by making promises which he keeps, by being even better than his word, by scouring his shame through heroic deeds, by becoming at last fully himself— the son who frees himself from Bolingbroke's time—is permitted not the tragic route of bloody revenge or a similar irreversible action but the comical-historical-epical route of self-transcendence.

Throughout *Henry IV, Part One,* Hal is also lucky in that he appears to be worse than he is rather than, like some of the villains of tragedy, better than he is. Hal's task is to raze out rotten opinion and symbolically to make up for Henry IV's crime. By bearing the burden of another guilt—a sin of omission—and then by reforming himself through action, Hal in effect also reforms the realm, for the Prince's reputation is the land's. The King has nightmare visions of Hal as his enemy or in Percy's pay and says that all men "Prophetically do forethink" Hal's fall (III.ii). But the King's image of the kind of prince Hal is and should become is uninformed and prescriptive. Hotspur, whom the King calls the theme of honor's tongue, extravagantly wishes to redeem honor by plucking it from moon or deep. Hal rejects both extremes and chooses a middle way, in which courage is tempered by common sense and courtesy. The king of crooked ways laments at the outset that Hal is not like Hotspur, "Amongst a grove the very straightest plant." But we come to see that Hal in *Henry IV* is a man of relaxed habits who mocks the Hotspur who would kill "some six or seven dozen of Scots at a breakfast."

In *Part Two,* the King's characterization of Hal suggests Falstaff and the ambiguity of the garden imagery:

> Most subject is the fattest soil to weeds,
> And he, the noble image of my youth,
> Is overspread with them.   (IV.iv.54)

The King does not know, as Ely tells us in *Henry V,* that

> The strawberry grows underneath the nettle,
> And wholesome berries thrive and ripen best
> Neighbor'd by fruit of baser quality.   (I.i.60)

In *Part Two,* Falstaff, who perpetually juxtaposes the heroic and the physical in ways which disintegrate the false heroic, tells us that Hal has manured the lean, sterile, and bare land of the Lancasters by drinking sherry. This is Falstaff's magical potion not only for the brain's nimble and fiery shapes but for Hal's becoming "hot and valiant" (IV.iv.103). Unlike that treacherous "sober-blooded boy," his brother John, Hal is a thin man who consorts with the fat, who tills his fat soil without being overwhelmed by weeds. In a play remarkable for its imagery of eating, Hal could be called the true devourer, as he is of Hotspur's honor, yet a man who never becomes fat. In this too he is unique. The King turns energy into power. He accuses Richard II of gorging men's eyes with his presence, but Henry himself has grown to so great a bulk that he swallows all love. Hotspur can only "taste" his horse; he turns energy prematurely into action. Falstaff is more complicated. He turns energy into the huge hill of flesh for which "the grave doth gape." But he also lards the lean earth and Hal's imagination during an unquiet time, for he turns energy into language. In this skill he is nearly invulnerable because he creates a play world almost winning enough to be taken for the real. By companioning Hal improbably with Falstaff, Shakespeare is attempting to hold up a mirror for magistrates which is more humane than that devised by moralists. It is a mirror for a prince who comes closer to being diverted through the green world of comedy than stuck in the rigid postures of tragedy. It is a mirror for a prince who at last freely pursues his own purposes through time and history. And yet, like other men of power, Hal sacrifices means to ends.

II

Behind *Henry IV, Part One* lies a long tradition of the prodigal son, for whom there is finally more joy in heaven and among prelates in *Henry V.* This archetypal success story is extremely useful dramatically, for in it Hal's kingship is twice delayed so that his experience as man can be deepened and his quality tested. In the legend, Shakespeare finds a rising line of action from vanity and riot to self-control, a movement which Shakespeare (and Hal) can exploit almost too cleverly. Hal, covering discretion with a coat of folly, and springing to life when men think least he will, has the theatrical sense of timing of the active politicians of the histories— Richard III and Bolingbroke. It is in managing his reputation that Hal seems the true son of his canny father. Henry IV tells Hal (III.ii) that as Bolingbroke he kept his person fresh and new so that "like a comet" he could be "wond'red at." Hal is even more effective than his father, for Hal does finally, as he promises in soliloquy, "falsify men's hopes," "show more goodly and attract more eyes." At times Hal exhibits something of the manipulative intelligence of even the villains in Shakespeare. In one of our essays, Danby calls Hal a machiavel of goodness. Hal knows almost too well how to turn past evils to advantages. Even when we remember that Shakespeare's heroes "stage" their careers, the note of calculation in Hal's playing the truant to chivalry so that his fault can be the foil to his reformation is disturbing. We might occasionally wonder what the difference is between the King's stepping a little higher than his vow, Falstaff's turning diseases to commodity, and Hal's using Percy as his factor to engross up glorious deeds. It is clear that the line in the histories between those who direct time, those whom time serves, and the time-servers is not as clearly defined as it is in the tragedies. But we emphasize the gap between Hal in soliloquy and among his friends, between the "true" Hal and Hal as seemer or player, at the peril of the play.

A. P. Rossiter sees the major characters in the histories as caught in a twilight world of contingencies and as subtragic. If seen from the vantage point of the tragedies, to be sure, Hal is not confronted with irresistible temptations, he is not bisected by the problems he confronts, and hence we could say that he does not face genuine choices. If only Hal, Hamlet-like, had spoken a second soliloquy to deepen or explain the first, we might say! For his "I know you all" speech is less a stage in an agony of self-conflict than a short-circuiting of conflict. From the outset, Hal is a man of clear will and purpose. His trials are poor equivalents for the shattering experiences Hamlet must undergo before he can collaborate with the ghost in fulfilling his mission. Hamlet, Hal's more complicated cousin and the most fully aware of the tragic heroes, is motivated by a ghost that is related to the providence attending the fall of sparrows, whereas Hal's mission, at least until *Henry V,* is wholly secular. To collaborate with destiny, Hamlet must make a series of painful discoveries concerning the limitations of mortality; indeed, he must perhaps change his very nature. No such devastating claims are made upon Hal. And yet the last play of the series celebrates the fact that Hal undergoes a transformation when he banishes Falstaff and a part of himself.

The Prince's "sin" of coveting honor or glory is tempered in *Part One* by the generosity with which, before Shrewsbury, he speaks Hotspur's "deservings like a chronicle" or with which he graces Falstaff when he permits the fat knight to claim for himself the death of Hotspur. Hal's virtues and follies here are acquainted with one another. But the man who in *Part One* is of all humors since the days of goodman Adam becomes the man in *Henry V* whose offending Adam is whipped out of him by consideration, that admirable and perhaps chilling virtue. As Hal moves from his role as clouded sun to that of the sun king, whose "liberal eye doth give to every one/Thawing cold fear" (Prologue IV.44), he leaves the realm of Falstaff and the men of the changing moon and water and enters something like the realm of air and fire invoked by the first chorus. Canterbury praises the new King, whose body now becomes "as a paradise/T' envelop and contain celestial spirits." The unweeded garden of the former histories has in the last been miraculously changed, both in terms of the King's body and the realm's. When reading *Henry IV*, we can neither ignore this later apotheosis of fallible Prince Hal no feed it back into the earlier plays. Prince Hal, to be sure, was always destined for something like epic, not tragic, status, in a tradition closer to that of kingdom-founding Aeneas than of doomed Achilles. History demanded this role and Shakespeare in *Henry V* makes an extraordinarily good case for it. But, as Granville-Barker has observed, *Henry V* is in ways a false lead for Shakespeare. The complexity of Brutus and Hamlet, tragic heroes of the same period, renders the two-dimensionality of King Henry V, so long tutored in ambiguities by Falstaff, surprising. The key to this simplicity lies in the rejection scene at the end of *Part Two*, in Hal's denial of his life with Falstaff.

III

Throughout two plays Shakespeare gives Hal, the man who is to become the most responsible king of the histories, the fellowship of the master verbal prestidigitator and escape artist of all comedy. Indeed, the only genius among Hal's tutors is a clown who paradoxically mocks all of the values Hal must live by, who is deaf to the hearing of "anything good." The severe Justice confronts Falstaff several times in *Part Two*, checking him roundly for not listening, for his "malady of not marking," and calling him a great fool. From the beginning of this play, which is introduced by Rumor, the Justice will not let Falstaff wrench the true cause the false way. Yet at the end of the play, Falstaff cries upon hearing that Hal is king, "Let us take any man's horses; the laws of England are at my commandment." Hal himself must finally challenge Falstaff's monstrous lies, as he did after Gadshill but not after Shrewsbury. From "I know you all" to "I know thee not, old man; fall to thy prayers," in the rejection scene we know that Hal has understood the unscrupulousness of Falstaff. The Prince could forgive a friend who saw all value, even honor, as a word, and all life, even in war, as a game, but the new King cannot.

As several of our essays indicate, the rejection of Falstaff can be interpreted as Hal's ultimately and rightly dismissing his reverend vice ("The tutor and the feeder of my riots"), as his betrayal of a friend ("The King has killed his heart"), or as his sacrifice of a way of life, now too costly for a king ("Banish plump Jack and banish all the world"). One group of readers justifies the rejection and emphasizes the necessity for Hal's exchanging private life for public duty. Another group is troubled and often emphasizes the continuity between the histories and the tragedies, where a similar rejection of friend by friend would not be condoned. Both interpretations have obvious validity. In 1597–98, in the context of the histories, the banishment of Falstaff seems inevitable. Towards the end of *Henry IV, Part Two,* however, the rhythms of a new rhetoric, of an almost high church language that becomes more organ-like in parts of *Henry V,* suggest that certain notes in the wide scale of values of *Henry IV, Part One* are now being silenced, others sounded very loud indeed. Whether we wish to call Shakespeare's process of isolating and elevating Hal here a denial of Hal's own complexity, white-washing, heroicizing, or the full realization of Hal's kingly potential, the apparent ease with which Hal masters all opposition clearly comes at a price. The energy and way of life which Hal banishes, however, emerge later in Shakespeare, where a creature of earth and water ascends more convincingly into air and fire.

There are teasing parallels between the way Shakespeare's late history plays give birth to his greatest comic creation and the way one of his late tragedies gives birth to Cleopatra, his greatest female protagonist. Both the knight who is out of all order, all compass, and the bewitching queen for whom Antony must find out new heaven, new earth, press to the limit the forms that contain them and seem to betoken new forms and new meanings. The knight and the queen are similar, as Jonas Barish points out, in their infinite variety and in the challenges they pose, in the most disturbing ways, to the values of the English and Roman establishments. This kind of vitality—as life-giving and yet treacherous as water—is finally rejected in 1597–98 but endowed with almost superhuman power in 1606–7. Antony, when leading the Egyptian bacchanals on Pompey's galley, and thus making the world go round in a fashion worthy of the Boar's Head, cries to Caesar—"Be a child o' th' time," and Caesar replies, "Possess it, I'll make answer" (II.vii.106). In the realm of the histories, Hal cannot permit himself to become the child of Falstaff or of life itself as fully as (in the world of tragic love) Antony can become Cleopatra's. Cleopatra makes hungry where most she satisfies, whereas Hal rejects Falstaff and his ways with an almost puritanical horror of the flesh:

> I have long dreamt of such a kind of man,
> So surfeit-swell'd, so old, and so profane;
> But, being awak'd, I do despise my dream.
> Make less thy body hence, and more thy grace.
>
> *(Part Two:* V.v.53)

Hal dismisses the gross fat man as sternly as Hamlet rejects the things rank and gross in nature that possess the unweeded garden. But Falstaff also represents qualities of love and life that are otherwise lacking in Hal's experience. Hal does banish part of the world with Falstaff, whereas Antony, for a love which he defines as the "nobleness of life," declares all kingdoms clay and the world well lost. Hal, thinking that he is at last fully awakened from nightmare, despises the long "dream" of his friendship with Falstaff, whereas Cleopatra, seeing clearly after the death of Antony for perhaps the first time, celebrates her dream of the emperor in whose bounty there was no winter. With the help of Cleopatra, Antony takes supreme risks with life and thus teaches us everything about the glory and limitations of our mortality. Hal is never trapped by, and thus never tests, strong toils of grace like Cleopatra's. The royal grace of the mirror of all Christian kings seems by comparison more a gift of nature than an achievement. Perhaps only Falstaff's laughter and intelligence could throw into perspective the world of the histories, in which all power tends to become policy. And perhaps only Cleopatra's imagination could open a vista from tragedy into the more hopeful world of great creating nature of the last romances, a world in which the banished are restored, Prospero acknowledges even Caliban as his own, time and history are transcended, and dreams create a new reality.

PART ONE

Interpretations

Falstaff, the Prince, and the History Play

by Harold E. Toliver

A rational eighteenth-century man of letters such as Maurice Morgann would undoubtedly bristle a little at our abandon in destroying his premises. He would have difficulty recognizing our portraits of Henry IV, for example, whom, in his simplicity, he had thought to be a rather impressive king despite a certain weakness at first for another man's crown. And he would be even more mystified by Henry V as Machiavellian strong-man and confused warmaker. Ignorant of Frazer and Freud, he would not think to look for the key to the complexity and interest of Falstaff, the "whoreson, obscene, greasy tallow-catch," in ritualistic and magical analogues;[1] he would probably want to ask whether critics ought to be getting into such things in the first place, and if so, how the a-rational elements of motivation, imagery, and symbolic action, if they exist, can be made intelligible. For when we consider these elements, the discussion of "character" in the sense of certain definite traits appears extremely limited; questions such as whether or not Falstaff is a coward are not important in themselves, and the facts were never really facts anyway. And concepts of form naturally grow more uncertain as response to character shifts. Hence, the question of what *kind* the history play belongs to can no longer be answered

From "Falstaff, the Prince, and the History Play," by Harold E. Toliver. From Shakespeare Quarterly, XVI (Winter, 1965), 63–66. Copyright © 1965 by the Shakespeare Association of America, Inc. Reprinted by permission of the author and publisher.

[1] See C. L. Barber's essay, "Saturnalia in the Henriad," which is printed in *Shakespeare: Modern Essays in Criticism,* ed. Leonard F. Dean (New York, 1957), pp. 169–91, and in *Shakespeare's Festive Comedy.* Cf. J. I. M. Stewart, *Character and Motive in Shakespeare* (Bristol, 1949), p. 127; Northrop Frye, "The Argument of Comedy," *English Institute Essays* (1949), p. 71; and Philip Williams, "The Birth and Death of Falstaff Reconsidered," *SQ,* VIII (1957), 359–65.

in strictly Aristotelian terms.[2] Once over the initial shock, however, the traditional rationalist might discover certain fruitful interactions between his approach to the history play and modern approaches. In the matter of the relative place of comic and heroic figures in the history play, for example, the neoclassicist's sense of "decorum"—of a form following certain laws of plot, character, and language—might be made to engage more profoundly the raw stuff of the human psyche and its institutions and rituals imitated in the form. And in return, we might have to admit that while it may not be necessary for all purposes to read history plays under the auspices of a category, we gain from being aware that they are not simply studies in isolated problems of motivation, or fragments of primitive ritual. They do indeed have "form," as some kings have "character." Approaching the history play through either perspective by itself is likely to leave us unsatisfied, as though we had gone hunting kudu and flushed jerboa.

For the history play at its best attempts to do more than evoke purely chauvinistic emotion through heroic pageantry and spectacle, as it was once assumed; and it is not totally incapable of containing its Saturnalian kings of misrule and its Oedipal overtones in a form that transcends and orders them. Shakespeare, at least, appears to have sought in the history play a fresh artistic form capable of integrating providential order, pragmatic political concerns, and

[2] The most complete attempts to arrive at a working concept of the history play *sui generis* are Irving Ribner's "The Tudor History Play: An Essay in Definition," *PMLA*, LXIX (1954), 591–609 and *The English History Play in the Age of Shakespeare* (Princeton University Press, 1957), pp. 1–32; H. B. Charlton's *Shakespeare: Politics and Politicians*, The English Association Pamphlet no. 72 (1929), pp. 7, 11, 13; Una Ellis-Fermor, *The Frontiers of Drama* (London, 1945), pp. 5–14, 34–55; Felix Schelling, *The English Chronicle Play* (New York, 1902); G. K. Hunter, "Shakespeare's Politics and the Rejection of Falstaff," *Critical Quarterly*, I (1959), 229–36. See also Coleridge's *Literary Remains*, H. N. Coleridge, ed. (London, 1836), VI, 160 ff.; A. C. Bradley, *Oxford Lectures on Poetry* (London, 1909), pp. 247–75; John Palmer, *Political Characters of Shakespeare* (London, 1945), pp. 184 ff.; W. H. Auden, "The Fallen City: Some Reflections on Shakespeare's *Henry IV*," *Encounter*, XIII, no. 5 (1959), 25; and, of course, Maurice Morgann, *An Essay on the Dramtic Character of Sir John Falstaff*, first published in 1777. Northrop Frye's *Anatomy of Criticism* is stimulating as usual, especially the following remarks: "The History merges so gradually into tragedy that we often cannot be sure when communion has turned into catharsis," and "The central theme of Elizabethan history is the unifying of the nation and the binding of the audience into the myth as the inheritors of that unity, set over against the disasters of civil war and weak leadership" (pp. 283–84). Finally, A. P. Rossiter's brief book *English Drama from Early Times to the Elizabethans* (London, 1950) illuminates the "mungrell" forms brilliantly, from an inclusive perspective. [See in this collection Barber, pp. 51–70, Bradley, pp. 71–77, and Frye, pp. 89–93.

timeless human impulses.[3] One of the primary effects of that integration is an adjustment between inner and outer worlds, both in the hero and, since the history play is more nationalistic and "rhetorical" than other dramatic forms, through the hero in the audience, didactically. In ethical matters, the adjustment is between the inner conscience and the amoral demands of political life; in economic motives, between personal and collective "property"; and in broadly social and religious matters, between the old Adam who rushes impulsively to Eastcheap and the redeemed Adam who takes his fixed place in the ranks or at Whitehall.

These adjustments involve the audience in a communal "rhythm" through a language generally more openly incantational than the language of Shakespearian tragedy and ritualistic in a different sense. For more than one kind of ritual and one kind of magic is involved in dramatic action. In a broad sense, "ritual" means any closely patterned visual ceremony or rhythmic language that engages the emotions of its participants and fuses them into a harmonious community. Both spectacle and rhythm work by raising like emotions throughout an audience and providing a common symbolic or "pulsing" medium for their transmission. Some rituals depend upon primitive forms of magic, and Falstaff, as J. I. M. Stewart, C. L. Barber, and Philip Williams believe, reflects certain fragments of them. But others become assimilated into sophisticated art and are consciously manipulated as one of its dimensions. In less primitive forms, they work not only through contact with highly charged currents from the subconscious, which criticism, as Morgann conceived of it, is ill-equipped to deal with, but also through a complex assortment of powers released by formal art. In the rejection scene, for example, the ritual of the new king depends upon the total of thematic, imagistic, and formal pressures brought to bear by the whole play or series of plays—and their social and political context. If tragic ritual reconciles the audience to a higher destiny of some sort, perhaps to the power of the gods or to a world of suffering beyond the protagonist's control, the ritual of the history play aims somewhat lower, at adjustment to political life—which may be thought to reveal destiny also, but destiny at least *filtered through* a social medium.

Social and political context is thus especially important in the

---

[3] Shakespeare's experimentation with the form is clear from the varieties he tried and from devices such as Rumour's induction to *2 Henry IV* (which suggests the uncertainty of historical events as experienced and yet offers the broader vision of the chronicler who sees everything with accuracy) and the chorus in *Henry V*, which moves the play toward dramatized epic.

history play, which in England developed under special historical conditions that caused it to rise and decline rapidly as literary types go. Though other dramatists experimented with it, Shakespeare (with the possible exception of the anonymous author of *Woodstock*) was the only one to see its full potential as a separate form. In his variation, it appealed strongly to an audience prepared to see it in a certain way, or in Mr. Barber's term, to "participate" in its special kind of ritualized nationalistic emotion. Like English tragedy, it arose partly out of the old morality and mystery plays; but onto these it grafted chronicle accounts of past events, folk-lore, native myth, and a new spirit of nationalism, all of which it shaped into moral patterns designed to bring out the providential guidance, the "meaning," of history. Since an audience removed from the original context cannot "participate" in historical ritual with the same intensity as an Elizabethan royalist who believed in the king's divine prerogatives, the historical context and content create problems that are less obtrusive in other dramatic forms, if present at all. But despite its inherent shortcomings, the history play at its best (in the series of plays from *Richard II* to *Henry V*) achieves an essentially new structure and dramatic rhythm, both peculiar to itself and effective.

Some aspects of that structure are borrowed from comedy and tragedy, and here again the neoclassicist, if put to the test, might be quick to see some aspects of the blend that others would overlook. Aristotle's concept of *anagnorisis* and *catharsis* would seem relevant, for example, in describing Falstaff's role as tragic victim—only one role among several, needless to say, but involved and crucial.[4] In one aspect the "plot" of *2 Henry IV* can be taken as a *mixed variation* of comic and tragic action, culminating in a sacrificial act with the new king acting as personal vicegerent for destiny. The effectiveness of the rejection speech as incantation depends upon our seeing the accumulated evidence as to the way of a world that Falstaff has affronted and does not fit, a world *requiring* a certain political order that cannot tolerate Falstaff as Chief Justice. The evidences of tragic form are clear enough before that, once we set aside the oversimplified notion that a figure must be either comic or tragic and not both. The implications of Falstaff's childlike self-love and hedonism from the beginning of *1 Henry IV* compose, in Francis Fergusson's Jamesian analogy, one of a set of "mirrors" reflecting

---

[4] This role has been mentioned occasionally but has not been extensively explored. See D. A. Traversi, *An Approach to Shakespeare* (New York, 1956), p. 32, and *Shakespeare from Richard II to Henry V* (Stanford University Press, 1957), pp. 77 ff.; Stewart, p. 127 ff.; Auden, p. 25; Williams, p. 363.

the central action, the search for an effective adjustment between
the inner self and the collective social organism. Since the aim of
this action is ultimately to "redeem time" (and thus to redeem the
times),[5] both in the sense of justifying "history" and in reconciling
the audience to its historical role, Falstaff is best seen as a rebel
against history, as guilty of *hubris* as he is of Saturnalian misrule.

[5] Cf. J. A. Bryant, Jr., "Prince Hal and the Ephesians," *Sewanee Review*, LXVII
(1959), 204–19; Benjamin T. Spencer, "*2 Henry IV* and the Theme of Time,"
UTQ, XIII (1944), 394–99; Paul A. Jorgensen, "'Redeeming Time' in Shakespeare's *Henry IV*," *Tennessee Studies in Literature*, V (1960), 101–9.

The Unity and Background
of *Henry IV, Part One*

by A. R. Humphreys

The Unity of the Play

Since Sir Edmund Chambers published *Shakespeare, A Survey* (1925), several critics have taken issue with his treatment of the *Henry IV*s. To query this treatment once again is not to undervalue his immense contribution to Shakespeare scholarship but it is to try to set in the right light plays on which a good many readers (fewer playgoers, perhaps) probably share Sir Edmund's views, expounded thus:

> In *Henry IV*, chronicle-history becomes little more than a tapestried hanging, dimly wrought with horsemen and footmen, in their alarums and excursions, which serves as a background to groups of living personages conceived in quite another spirit and belonging to a very different order of reality. . . . All this . . . becomes the setting of a single great comic figure, and thereby the plays attain the unity which their intermediate position in the cycle . . . makes it difficult for them to accomplish in any other way. Instead of the dynamic unity of an emotional issue set and resolved in the course of the action, they have the static unity of a pervading humorous personality.

This, however, is precisely the opposite of what one should say. Far from the history's being merely a "dimly wrought" background to "groups of living personages" of superior reality, the historical themes are urged upon us with Shakespeare's utmost vigour. As Hazlitt observed, "the heroic and serious part of these two plays . . .

"The Unity and Background of *Henry IV, Part One*" [editor's title]. *From "Introduction" by A. R. Humphreys to* The First Part of King Henry IV, *The Arden Shakespeare (London: Methuen & Co., Ltd., 1960; Cambridge, Mass.: Harvard University Press, 1960), pp. xxxix–lx. Copyright © 1960 by Methuen & Co., Ltd. Reprinted by permission of the publishers. The section on Falstaff has been transposed to the end of the selection.*

is not inferior to the comic and farcical." And far from the unity's being "static," confined to the dominance of Falstaff, it is dynamic, complex, and organized from a wonderful interrelationship of material, so that one agrees with Elizabeth Montagu—"I cannot help thinking that there is more of contrivance and care in the execution of this play than in almost any he has written" (*Essay on the Writings and Genius of Shakespear*, 1769, 100). The coexistence of comic and serious plots is not confined to their efficient alternation, though their alternations are superbly efficient. The more they are scrutinized, the more connected they appear, the connection being sometimes of parallelism and reinforcement, sometimes of antithesis and contrast, sometimes a reversal by which serious or comic is judged by the other's values. There are, too, stylistic relationships by which, for instance, major types of imagery are common to both parts, or by which the texture and pace of prose scenes offset those of verse.

At first sight, one takes the two plots to be antithetical—court against tavern, nobility against commonalty, energy against sloth, time-saving against time-wasting, gravity against wit, verse against prose, and so on. To a hasty view the play seems to split into separate strata. These two different kinds of thing do indeed furnish different parts of the mind, stretch it, and make it feel extended over a wide dichotomy. Yet closer study shows a different state of things—branches belonging to a single trunk. The first speech expresses a hope for national unity; this hope is equally denied by both plots, by the Percys' rising and Hal's insubordination. Both these troubles reflect on Henry's own conduct—they have a causal, not casual link with it, for the Percys, instruments of his usurpation, turn against him the very pretexts of national welfare on which his rise was based, and his own exclusion of the rightful heir (Mortimer) threatens to be repaid by a failure of the succession in Hal. Hal seems to Henry a replica of Richard II, for each man mingles his royalty with capering fools and enfeoffs himself to popularity, and the benefits Richard flung recklessly upon Henry, Hal is recklessly flinging away again. Both serious and comic plots show the usurping Henry dogged by retribution: over both plots hangs the hand of constituted authority—defeat and death for rebels, the gallows or banishment for wastrels. Both plots sound the theme of ambition and rapacity—Hotspur will "cavil on the ninth part of a hair" and is as eager to monopolize honour as Falstaff to discard it. There is as little principle among barons as among thieves; Hotspur can no more depend on his fellow-conspirators, from the "lack-brain" (II.iii.16) to Northumberland and Glen-

dower, than Falstaff on Hal and Poins or they on him. There are all
sorts of ways in which the two plots operate similarly; as the rebels'
self-seeking is masked by Hotspur's rhapsodies about honour, so the
rascals' exploits are romanticized (in their own eyes) by reference
to a world of legend, literature, and heroic service; Falstaff ideal-
izes highwaymen as vividly as sherris-sack—they are Diana's for-
esters, minions of the moon, governed like the sea by celestial
power (I.ii). When Hotspur rants about the Mortimer-Glendower
fight (I.iii), and Falstaff about the buckram men (II.iv), we think
the former heroic and the latter outrageous, yet to fail to see a relationship is to miss part of the fabric of linkage. Another parody-
relationship is that between the Falstaff-Hal burlesque (II.iv) and
the King's genuine reproof (III.ii). Similar motifs appear seriously
and comically; the Gad's Hill bustle is the comic counterpart of
Hotspur's insurrection; Falstaff's sanctimoniousness has its serious
echo in Henry's yearnings for a Crusade; the predatory campaign-
ing is both heroic and preposterous at once; and motifs of bodily
states and actions, and particularly of disease, run thematically
through both plots.

The interrelationships form an intricate web among the main
characters. The connections between King, Prince, Hotspur, and
Falstaff compel us to assess them this way and that, from which
arises the play's moral value. The King and Hotspur, for instance,
are similar (rivals in the same game), but also antithetical (authority versus rebellion); the King and Falstaff, again, are alike (fel-
lows in subversion, elderly examples for Hal), but also opposite
(rule against misrule). Hotspur and Falstaff are both examples for
Hal of rebellious anarchy, contrasting however by their differing
codes of conduct and honour. Falstaff and Hal are simultaneously
allies (boon companions, fellow-scoffers) and opponents (Vicious
Age, Virtuous Youth). Hotspur and Hal, apparently at opposite
extremes of promise, meet on the ground of youth and valour.
Finally, the King and Hal, apparently opposed, are of the same
family, and have in common their "policy." As Professor Empson
has said, much of the play's value lies in this dramatic "ambiguity"
which leaves one deliberating this way and that, for and against all
the main characters.[1]

The moral structure of the play is, as Quiller-Couch affirmed, a
morality-structure, the "Contention Between Vice and Virtue for
the Soul of a Prince," though it is much more also. It is worth noting

---

[1] "Fal. and Mr Dover Wilson," *Kenyon Review,* 1953, XV, 221. [Reprinted in
this collection, pp. 78–82.]

how the possibilities are organized around Hal. In a simple sense, Hotspur and Falstaff represent virtue and vice—the former the hero, blunt, honest, too active to be sensual, enchanted by honour; the latter his diametrical opposite. Yet merely opposite they are not; Hal cannot rule well by rejecting one model and following the other. Most importantly, he must inhabit the real world while they both live their fantasies. Both men are dangerously attractive, and their value to Hal is in showing what to seek (Hotspur's valour, Falstaff's ripeness), but equally what to avoid (Hotspur's recklessness, Falstaff's indulgence). Both subvert the decent conventions—Falstaff has no aim other than sensuality, Hotspur none other than battle. Both, Brooks and Heilman put it in *Understanding Drama,* "are *below* the serious concerns that fill the play"—they "do not stand quite on the level of the adult world where there are jobs to be done." To say that neither is serious enough sounds pedantic: who wants a serious Hotspur, a serious Falstaff? Why not love their brilliant displays of life? Yet it is fundamental in both men that neither can see things in proportion: Hotspur's imagination starts away from good judgement as fast as Falstaff's. His greed for honour is for monopoly; he aims only at war; he is as much a liability as an asset to his allies.[2]

As for Hal, midpoint between, he reflects on these plots and codes of life. Noncommittally poised, he provokes the maximum dramatic expectation. It is to protract this expectation that though the King and he are reconciled in Part One the process has to be repeated in Part Two as though Part One had not occurred—the Prince still a companion to the common streets, the King mindless of his virtues. Part Two provides the matching half of a diptych, Hal's committal to gravity (the Lord Chief Justice) after frivolity. His prior "loose behaviour" is a nodus of both serious and comic plots; Hotspur and the King, on their level, and Falstaff, on his, are all punished for misreading him.

As Hotspur and Falstaff stand opposed to Hal as excess and defect of Honour, so the King and Falstaff stand as opposed versions of Age and Authority, responsible and irresponsible, but both blemished by Anarchy. Brooks and Heilman observe that in taking the King off in the tavern play Falstaff parodies not only Euphuism but "the kind of seriousness with which authority has to express, and take, itself; the carefully balanced antitheses, the allusions to natural history, the appeal to learned authorities, the laboured truism"; and it is this mocked authority which Hal (his father's rep-

[2] See [the Arden edition] V.iv.119, note, for a comment on rash valour.

resentative as well as his mocker) ominously retorts upon Falstaff.

Yet these versions of authority, however opposed, are not simple antitheses. Hal reaches kingly success by combining and transcending them. To his father's masterfulness he adds Falstaff's broad humanity, so that when king he commands not only "culled and choice-drawn cavaliers" but "all the good lads in Eastcheap." The King and Falstaff are complementary.

Moreover, both have a double function for Hal. On the face of it, the King stands for rule, Falstaff for misrule, and Falstaff, like the rebel lords, is to be suppressed. Yet Henry stands for rule only because he has himself rebelled—the laws of England have been at his command as Falstaff expects them to be at his, and woe to the due succession. So Hal sees in Henry both regal firmness and regal weariness: kingship is a glory but a burden.

Falstaff's function is more subtly dual. Anarchic though he is, he gives Hal much of value, not only negatively (showing how not to act) but positively. Professor Empson has made this point well:

> The idea is not simply that Falstaff is debauched and tricky, though that in itself made him give Hal experience . . . but that he had the breadth of mind and social understanding which the Magnanimous Man needed to acquire. . . . Indeed, if you compare Hal to his brother and father, whom the plays describe so unflinchingly, it is surely obvious that to love Falstaff was a liberal education.[3]

Falstaff indeed makes the point himself in relating how "excellent endeavour of drinking good and good store of fertile sherris" has in Hal warmed the cold Bolingbrokian blood. However much Falstaff owes to the morality Vice, his function in respect of kingship is much more than that of mere tempter.

Serious and comic themes are entwined by many other echoes and links. They unite in a vision of national life both broad and deep, and are expressed in a style of extraordinary energy, whether in serious verse or comic prose. This vision of national life has its comprehensive geographical range and its long perspectives of time; it looks into the future and it reaches into the past, for retrospection is as integral to reminiscences of a comic past[4] as to those of tragic history. The great idea of England is woven from all these themes.

The structural coherence is equally organic. The Qq's lack of scene-division makes evident the play's perpetual counterpointing. There are such interactions as that between what are now I.i and I.ii: the former, in pressing strenuous verse, treats of mental and

---

[3] "Fal. and Mr Dover Wilson," *Kenyon Review*, 1953, XV, 246–56.
[4] Cf. *1H4*, II.iv.310–12, 325–28; *2H4*, III.ii, passim.

bodily strain, the country's dangers, the swift succession of military events; its emotions are grave, troubled, angry, its pace increasingly swift. I.ii in lavish comic prose is the entire antithesis; time, speed, and the making of appointments are rejected for timeless leisure; strung nerves give place to unbuttoned slumber; combat and worry yield to capons and wenches. Yet both express disorder and a prince's misconduct; in both a campaign is prepared—defiance to the Percys, robbery at Gad's Hill; and Hal's soliloquy at the end of I.ii knots both together. II.ii and II.iii are also related: the comic violence of Gad's Hill leads on to Hotspur's military exuberance— indeed, each scene sets forth its hero soliloquizing in exasperation at perfidious associates. In IV.i and IV.ii, we first have Vernon's great speech about the Prince's panoply and then meet Falstaff equally bound for war but scandalously cynical about his tattered men. The counterpointing is obvious, and rich; it would not need mentioning were the unity of the play more generally recognized. And finally, in this structural aspect, one notices that serious and comic plots, at first in quite different spheres, are progressively brought together. As the rebellion moves to its climax, Hal emerges from comic folly into serious leadership, and the comic scenes show every cognizance of the serious. Both are borne along on the tide running to Shrewsbury, and on the battlefield both attitudes to life are put to the test. The battle, however awkward on the stage, is the thematic resolution: Hal dispels the fears about him, Hotspur is proved to have been overweening, kingship is confirmed, and Falstaff is suddenly shown in a shocking light as he stabs the dead Hotspur. Shrewsbury is the touchstone which tries men and causes by Part One's criterion of prowess.

The Historical Outlook

In a discussion of Shakespeare's increasingly secular historical outlook, by which the "absolute moral values" of the *Henry VI– Richard III* series change into the Erastian criteria of *Henry IV– Henry V*, Professor John Danby offers a brilliant interpretation of the *Henry IV*s.[5] Instead of a kingdom, however evil, under God— which he takes to be the "vision" of the earlier sequence—he finds here one governed by purely secular motives of expediency and "Commodity," a morally sordid state however vigorous its physical

[5] *Sh.'s Doctrine of Nature*, 1949, pp. 81–101. [Reprinted in this collection, pp. 93–96.]

life. Earlier, the issues had been "Is the King right or wrong? Is the state just or unjust?" Now, he avers, "the questions are reduced and vulgarized: Is the King strong or weak? Is the state secure or insecure?"

The difference between the sequences can easily be exaggerated; nevertheless it exists. Shakespeare's political instincts seem to have swung like a pendulum. In the first sequence, however selfish the actions of most of the characters (and supremely of Richard III), the presiding assumption is of divine superintendence, punishing sin. In the second, though this assumption is conventionally recognized, and Henry V puts himself religiously in the right, it lacks force. In *Macbeth* and *King Lear,* however, it more than regains its strength; both plays are myths expressing the religious conflict of moral law and moral anarchy.

The *Henry IV*s inhabit the Tudor Erastian world. Religious references are mostly perfunctory. Henry's wish for a crusade, true though it seems in Part One, appears questionable in Part Two (*2H4,* IV.v.208–11). The rebels make much of Bolingbroke's gospel-sworn and broken oath, yet they themselves are parties to the guilt. In Part Two Westmoreland urges the traditional sanctities against the Archbishop's rising (*2H4,* IV.i), but is answered with political necessity. Prince John's "God, and not we, hath safely fought to-day" (*2H4,* IV.ii.122) frankly assimilates God to the wiles of state. The most striking sign of secularism is the King's rebound from remorseful reminiscence—for which one expects a moralizing conclusion—to a purely practical resolution (*2H4,* III.i.92–93):

> Are these things then necessities?
> Then let us meet them like necessities.

Despite themes of sin and expiation the plays develop in terms not of a supernatural metaphysic of history but of the practical ends of worldly action; they reflect a necessitarian view of political action, a sense of compelling reality. Some qualifications, admittedly, should be made to this. Religious sanctions are not entirely superceded; Carlisle's prophesied disasters come to pass (*R2,* IV.i.114 ff.); Henry IV suffers remorse; Henry V makes expiation (*H5,* IV.i.312–25). But the effect is casual, and Dover Wilson rightly warns us not to overlay the *Richard II–Henry V* sequence with too much moralizing.[6] In this respect the chronicles point the way; they mostly perform a straddle by which they show Richard II as a bad king though they also lament his misfortunes and downfall, so that

[6] *Sh.'s Histories at Stratford,* 1951, 18–19.

they condemn his follies yet extract emotion from his sufferings.[7]
Shakespeare follows Holinshed who, while moralizing on sin and
remorse (e.g., "A guiltie conscience in extremitie of sicknesse pinch-
eth sore"), commits himself no more to Richard II than to Henry
and, whatever emotion he derives from Henry's unquiet time, keeps
the story secular. Henry's conscience troubles him, but mainly with
a worried sense that his course was inevitable ("That I and greatness
were compell'd to kiss": *2H4*, III.i.74). To the question of *why*
Henry's was an unquiet time the answer is that his abettors were
unruly rather than that God was outraged; and to the question *why*
they were unruly the answer is that they were ambitious rather than
that the moral order was flouted (though flouted it certainly was).

Dr. Irving Ribner has questioned whether Shakespeare deeply
meant to show divine punishment for Richard's deposition.[8] If such
punishment were the lesson of *Richard II,* why did Essex's followers
launch their rebellion by having the play performed? Why publicize
sacrilege? It is true that in the long run, interpreted by the "Tudor
myth," Bolingbroke's crime resulted in divinely-prompted wars until
exorcised in the blessed union of Lancastrian Henry VII and his
Yorkist queen. But the second tetralogy looks less towards the remote *terminus ad quem* of the Tudor accession, however sanctified,
than to the climax of Henry V's victories, and though *Henry V* is
not without religious feeling that feeling is hardly distinguished
from patriotic rant. Even in the *Henry IV*s the shadow of retribution does not prevent Henry's being the centre of authority and the
rightful suppressor of rebellion.

Henry IV's career, then, proclaims less that God punishes deposition than that the king must rule. This was a sixteenth-century
theme. Much as the Elizabethans execrated Machiavelli, he fas-
cinated them by his cool recommendations of "policy." But even
without Machiavelli the importance of rule was evident in the
collapse of feudalism. Ribner quotes Tyndale's *Obedience of a
Christian Man* (1528; ed. Locett, 1885, 93–94):

> Yea, and it is better to have a tyrant unto thy king than a shadow: a
> passive king that doth nought himself but suffreth other to do with
> him what they will and to lead him whither they list. For a tyrant,
> though he do wrong unto the good, yet he punisheth the evil, and
> maketh all men obey, neither suffreth any man to poll but himself
> only. A king that is soft as silk and effeminate, that is to say turned

---

[7] The fifth story in *A Myrroure for Magistrates* is headed "Howe kyng Richarde
the seconde was for his euyll gouernaunce deposed from his seat, and miserably
murdred in prison."

[8] "The Political Problem in Sh.'s Lancastrian Tetralogy," *SP*, 1952, 171–84.

unto the nature of a woman—what with his own lusts, which are the
longing of a woman with child, so that he cannot resist them, and
what with the wily tyranny of them that ever rule him—shall be
much more grievous unto the realm than a right tyrant. Read the
chronicles and thou shalt find it ever so.

That describes the difference between Richard II and Henry IV, and
Shakespeare shows Henry's efficiency. In the Bagot-Aumerle quarrel (*R2*, IV.i.1–106) Henry dominates a situation such as Richard
had bungled with Mowbray and Bolingbroke; over Aumerle and
his conspiracy (which, be it noted, favours the "legitimate" king;
R2, V.ii–iii) he combines strength and mercy. In *2 Henry IV* the
rebels fail even though led by an Archbishop who displays "the
blood/Of fair King Richard, scrap'd from Pomfret stones" (*2H4*,
I.i.204–5). Richard falls through his own folly and injustice, climaxed
in the murder of the patriotic Gloucester (cf. *R2*, I.ii.1–3), which is
the subject of the *Myrroure for Magistrates'* third story[9] and the
crux of *Woodstock*. Bolingbroke rises rather on the Wheel of Fortune than by wicked purpose. In *Richard II* the "formal and ceremonial" quality of which Dr. Tillyard writes,[10] the ritualistic character
which Pater distinguishes,[11] mask the secular situation behind
poetry and symbolism; but peeping from behind the ritual and
ceremony there is, even here, the problem of efficient rule. And in
the *Henry IV*s this secular interest reduces the religious sentiment
to subordination, just as it heightens the realistic interest of lifelike
men competing in the world of action.

The Spirit of the Play

Professor Danby's analysis, however, goes beyond a mere assertion
of secularism to a striking characterization of the *Henry IV*s which
holds that they present a nation "disintegrated into mutually exclusive spheres"—Court, tavern, dissidents, country fusspots—motivated by "frigid opportunism, riotous irresponsibility, fatuous in-
consequence, quarrelsome 'honour'—with no common term except
the disease of each." " 'England,' " the argument continues,

> is sometimes said to be the heroic composite thing that is portrayed.
> If this is so, it is an England seen in her most unflattering aspects—

[9] "Howe syr Thomas Duke of Wudstocke Duke of Glocester, vncle to king
Richarde the seconde, was vnlawfully murdred."
[10] E. M. W. Tillyard, *Sh.'s History Plays*, 1944, 245.
[11] "Sh.'s English Kings," in *Appreciations*.

an England pervaded throughout court, tavern, and country retreat by pitiless fraud.

Falstaff's unscrupulousness is the code by which all live—"if anything unifies this congeries of monads it is 'Commodity.'" "Order" represents not Right, not God's Will, but effective Power: "Disorder" is not Unrighteousness, but secular Greed. So, Professor Danby concludes,

> Analysis leaves us, then, with symbols of Power and Appetite as the keys to the play's meaning: Power and Appetite the two sides of Commodity. . . . The England depicted in *Henry IV* . . . is neither ideally ordered nor happy. It is an England, on the one side, of bawdy house and thieves' kitchen, of waylaid merchants, badgered and bewildered Justices, and a peasantry wretched, betrayed, and recruited for the wars: an England, on the other side, of the chivalrous wolf-pack . . . and of state-sponsored treachery, in the person of Prince John—the whole presided over by a sick King, hag-ridden by conscience, dreaming of a Crusade to the Holy Land as Monsieur Remorse thinks of slimming and repentance. Those who see the world of *Henry IV* as some vital, joyous, Renaissance England must go behind the facts that Shakespeare presents. It is a world where to be normal is to be anti-social, and to be social is to be anti-human. Humanity is split in two. One half is banished to an underworld where dignity and decency must inevitably submerge in brutality and riot. The other half is restricted to an over-world where the same dignity and decency succumb to heartlessness and frigidity.

If this were so, the play's unity would be a unity of moral chaos, an Elizabethan *Waste Land*. Professor Danby offers this not as a total view of the play, whose inventive vitality he fully admits, but merely of its themes, and even then only insofar as they reflect Shakespeare's increasing secularism. Yet, if this is offered as the play's tenor, even with these qualifications, one must reply that Shakespeare was not Ben Jonson, that the *Henry IV*s (particularly Part One) are not *Volpone*, and that, related to the moralities though they are, this is not their true theme. Interpretations of this kind, it has been observed, "make a shambles of the heroic moments in the play, make them impossible to act." [12] Secular and realistic the plays have been admitted to be, and most of the characters are self-seeking, but their whole tenor forbids any summing-up in terms of mere greed. In a *Scrutiny* essay in 1934 Professor L. C. Knights (preceded by Ulrici in 1839, and followed by Professor Kenneth Muir in 1951) observed that in *1 Henry IV* "the Falstaff attitude is

[12] C. L. Barber, "From Ritual to Comedy," 30 (in *English Stage Comedy*, ed. W. K. Wimsatt, 1955). [Reprinted in this collection, pp. 51–70.]

in solution, as it were, throughout the play," but pointed out also that "a set of complementary impulses is also brought into play." In other words, though Falstaff is, to quote Professor Muir, "a living criticism of the world of 'policy,'" satirizing the gulf between precept and practice in the world of rank, he has anything but the last word on the values of life.

But how does this happen? Surely not, as it were, antiseptically, by our being so faced with the spectacle of corruption that our codes of virtue are reinforced. Falstaff may be what Ulrici called him, "the personified parody on the corrupt state of the chivalry and vassalry of the day," just as the chivalry's and vassalry's self-seeking throws into relief his hedonism. But should we feel the plays in this puritan-critical way? Surely not. Serious and comic do not reduce each other to shams; serious history enlarges itself to compass broad comedy, and comedy contributes more than mockery to our sense of history. "The heroic drama," Mr. Mark Van Doren has said of these plays,

> is modified by gigantic mockery, by the roared voice of truth; but the result is more rather than less reality, just as a cathedral, instead of being demolished by merriment among its aisles, stands more august.
>
> (*Shakespeare*, 139, 116)

The greatness of the *Henry IV*s lies in their not taking a disapproving view. To quote Mr. C. L. Barber again, "the dynamic relation of comedy and serious action is saturnalian rather than satiric." By the complex of cross-relationships that link together (as well as set off) the worlds of comedy and history one is left fully aware of human failings and yet impressed with great positives. The responsibilities of kingship, the honour of courage, the validity of justice, the energies of life, the zest of wit—these the plays fully assert, even though Henry is a usurper, Hotspur a firebrand, Hal a calculator, Falstaff a rogue. Fallible the persons may be, but their weaknesses are not what Shakespeare leaves uppermost in our minds. The Eastcheap comedy cannot be written down as "bawdy house and thieves' kitchen," that of Gad's Hill as "waylaid merchants," that of Gloucestershire as "badgered and bewildered Justices," even that of Falstaff's recruitment as "a peasantry wretched, betrayed, and recruited for the wars." Nor can the history be only the sum of chivalrous wolf-pack, state-sponsored treachery, and hag-ridden King, though it includes those elements. Shakespeare, one feels sure, would have been startled at the idea. Usurper, yes; but Henry is an effective king. Firebrand, yes; but Hotspur is a true hero. Hal calculates, but becomes a good king; Falstaff is a rogue, yet he warms the heart. The fundamental Shakespearean fact is that at Eastcheap there is communal happiness as well as trickery; at Gad's Hill, mirth as well as robbery (and is anyone a ha'p'orth the worse?); in Gloucestershire, rustic comedy as well as bewilderment; in the re-cruitment, Feeble's courage as well as Falstaff's corruption. Hotspur deserves the great tribute his wife pays (*2H4*, II.iii.18 ff.): state policy saves the nation: the King exerts a proper authority. The old view which sliced the play into independent alternating spectacles of politics and comedy was too casual, but the later one which inter-prets it through "the most serious ethical scrutiny" is too narrow. The play stands ethical scrutiny—that is its moral greatness—but it promotes a response of which moral sums are only a small part and moral didacticism abstracted from the rich dramatic context no part at all.[13] Shakespeare is not Jonson: cakes and ale exist along-side virtue. Instead of a morally-corrective partial vision there is a wise inclusive vision, derived from a true understanding of what men are like; in this, a judgment of what they should be like takes only a secondary place. "*Henry IV* is Shakespeare's vision of the 'happy breed of men' that was his England." Dover Wilson's view, expressed thus in his edition of *1 Henry IV*, is too roseate (it is, however, adjusted in *The Fortunes of Falstaff*), but it shows a proper sympathy with what is going on. Shakespeare loves his creatures (most of them, anyway) before he judges them; his story demands rebels and buffoons, but he thinks only on men.

The best analysis of this unified vision—the vision of many, various, interrelated modes and codes of life—is Cleanth Brooks's and Robert B. Heilman's.

> For the reader for whom the play does achieve a significant unity it may well seem that here Shakespeare has given us one of the wisest and fullest commentaries on human action possible to the comic mode —a view which scants nothing, which covers up nothing, and which takes into account in making its affirmations the most searching criti-cism of that which is affirmed. For such a reader, Shakespeare has no easy moral to draw, no simple generalization to make. . . . The world which Shakespeare portrays here is a world of contradictions—of mix-tures of good and evil. His vision of that world is ultimately a comic vision. . . . For the comic writer does not attempt to transcend the world of compromises, even though the more thoughtful writers of comedy, as here, may be fully aware of the seriousness of the issues. Comedy, after all, does not treat the lives of saints or heroes: it does

[13] This is not meant to imply for a moment that Professor Danby would, if giving a full critical account, wish to abstract "moral didacticism" from the "rich dramatic context."

not attempt to portray the absolute commitment to ultimate issues—
the total commitment which transcends, tragically and heroically, the
everyday world that we know. Shakespeare does not represent Prince
Hal (as he might conceivably do in a tragic treatment) as a callous
man, the scion of the "vile politician Bolingbroke." Hal will make a
good ruler, and Falstaff would undoubtedly make a very bad ruler.
Nor, on the other hand, is Falstaff portrayed as a villain: Falstaff too
has his case. Falstaff's wit—most of it at least—is not merely amusing
trifling. It constitutes a criticism of the world of serious affairs, a
criticism which, on certain levels, is thoroughly valid. The rulers of
the world had better not leave it totally out of account.[14]

Shakespeare has it both ways, all ways—for and against Henry,
Hal, Hotspur, Falstaff, court-life, tavern-life, the thirst for battle,
the thirst for sack. So does life.

Yet this needs some qualification. Shakespeare is not here writing
a problem play, leaving it doubtful which modes of action are to
be preferred. Were it otherwise, the argument that the *Henry IV*s
are related to the morality tradition would fall to the ground.
There is history here, as well as comedy—history which requires
responsible action. There are heroes here too, not superhuman
heroes but men who, having chosen their courses, must stand boldly
by them. Nature can be amoral. Comedy can, if it wishes, be
infinitely tolerant. But Shakespeare here is neither, wide though
his humanity shows itself. By understanding all points of view he
enables choices to be made in the light of full knowledge. He sets
virtues and vices in valid relationship; "the web of our life is of a
mingled yarn, good and ill together," *All's Well* was to proclaim.
The maturity of choice comes not from seeing life in black and
white but from knowing its manifold shades and then choosing
well. Shakespeare, undoctrinaire though he may be, is not Laodi-
cean; he upholds good government, in the macrocosm of the state,
and the microcosm of man. His vision is of men living, however
conflictingly, in a nation, a political-moral family, in a world of
moral choices (a testing-ground of conduct), in mutual relationships
which make their existence interesting and valuable. Life moves
by mixed impulses but not, on the whole, corrupt ones; it animates,
it challenges spirit and body to activity. To Chaucer, even the
Pardoner's rascality was delightful in its wholeheartedness; to Keats,
even a street-quarrel was beautiful, such energy did it release. To
Shakespeare, the usurper, the rebel, the intriguer, the credulous
wizard, the toper, and the rest are not parts of a disintegrated

[14] *Understanding Drama*, 1946, 386–87.

vulpine world. They combine in a totality which affirms the worth, the wealth, of living.

The Imaginative Impact

The play is about adventure—the adventure of conflict, the adventure of Bohemianism. It is consequently also about danger—the danger of defeat, the danger of retribution. And it is consequently also about courage—the courage of self-assertion, the courage of disreputability (Falstaff may be a physical coward but he is not a moral one, else he could not swim so buoyantly in his chosen element). It is therefore a very active play, and its style conveys its activity.

When Bernard Shaw observes that it shows "neither subtlety nor (for Shakespeare) much poetry in the presentation of the characters" [15] one must ask what he thinks poetry is. There is admittedly little of the lyrical-romantic (though cf. III.i.194–220), or of the tragic-profound (though cf. V.iv.76–82); nor does the action stop for set-pieces.[16] But almost every line works freshly and vivaciously in a spirited idiom which, like Hotspur's resolution,

> lends a lustre and more great opinion,
> A larger dare to our great enterprise.

And this is its poetry, the poetry of men in action.

The play insists on physical expressions and actions as these reflect emotions and tempers. From the outset the serious scenes sound a running theme of physical stress and strenuousness; the King and nation are shaken and wan with care, and frighted peace pants out short-winded accents of new broils. Foes confront each other with hostile paces and opposed eyes, with danger and disobedience showing in the moody frontiers of their brows. The defiance between Henry and the Percys, particularly Hotspur's speech on the popinjay lord, is packed with these physical portrayals (I.iii); so is Henry's comparison of Richard and himself (III.ii). As for the comic scenes, it is almost sufficient to remark that the centre of them is Falstaff; no dramatic figure makes more of physical bulk, condition, and behavior, as these express the nature of the

---

[15] *Dramatic Opinions*, 1906, 426.
[16] Such "pieces" as the "popinjay" speech (I.iii) or Henry's retrospect (III.ii) are off-stage portions of the action; and Hotspur's passage on Honour is a recognized extravagance, in character.

man, eating, drinking, sleeping, reporting the "wards, blows, ex-
tremities" of mock-heroism, flattering himself on "a cheerful look, a
pleasing eye, and a most noble carriage."

The point needs no labouring; the play abundantly annotates
emotions and behavior as expressed physically. As is habitual
with Shakespeare, states of mind are presented concretely; peace is
frighted and pants, the edge of war cuts his master, haste is hot in
question, news is uneven or smooth, riot and dishonour stain the
brow, the humour of idleness is unyoked, reformation glitters o'er
a fault, and so on. Again as is habitual with Shakespeare, animal
imagery gives an active and vivid precision; Hotspur prunes himself, bristles up the crest of youth, is wasp-stung, stung with pismires,
more splenetic than a weasel; the lord is a popinjay, Henry a
fawning greyhound; Falstaff's recruits fear gunshot worse than a
struck fowl or a hurt wild-duck. And, supremely, Hal and his
fellow-knights are plumed like estridges, bate like newly-bathed
eagles, are wanton as youthful goats and wild as young bulls. This
is the normal Shakespearean vitality, but never does it more vividly
create a real, physical, life.

This reality is enriched by a wealth of off-stage incident, and of
imaginatively-evoked social detail. Images of daily life abound; the
inn-yard is full of them (II.i); so are the tavern-scenes with their
banter and "unsavoury similes"; Hotspur uses them to scoff at
Glendower's poetry (III.i.122–58) or to chaff Lady Percy (III.i.241–
54). Falstaff indeed is presented in a context of meat and drink; he
is chops, fat-kidneyed, brawn, ribs, tallow, sweet beef, fat as butter,
a roasted Manningtree ox with a pudding in his belly, and he lards
the lean earth. The comic scenes have an ample offstage context,
of habitual hedonism in the company of underskinkers, drawers,
and all the good lads in Eastcheap, subject to the reproof of the
virtuous. We never in Part One see Falstaff's recruited ragamuffins,
discarded unjust servingmen and the like, but they are as vivid to
our minds as if they trooped before us. We glimpse the comic past,
too—the two-and-thirty years Falstaff has maintained Bardolph's
nose, the eighteen years' history of Bardolph's blushing, the time
when, at Hal's age, Falstaff could have crept into any alderman's
thumb-ring, the time when he had not forgotten what the inside of
a church looked like. This rich embedding in social life is helped
by the abundance of current and proverbial tags, of traditional
similes and ejaculations—fragments of highwaymen's shouts, of
ballads, or popular mythology, of romance-reading, of morality
plays and religious devotion. The serious action, too, is compassed
about with a great cloud of witnesses and of supporting actions;

there are military disasters and successes reported from Wales and
Scotland, Hotspur's popinjay-lord quarrel, and his restless sleep as
Lady Percy describes it, long and repeated historical retrospects
(III.ii; IV.iii; V.i), and the setting of a seething nation (I.i; I.iii;
II.iii; II.iv.329–67; III.ii; IV.ii; V.i). Armies clash, or march united;
messengers arrive and depart. The impression of public importance
is overwhelming; after all, the main serious concerns are the fate of
kingdoms and the quest for honour (the latter here equated with
public admiration). Personal actions encounter public comment;
Richard's deposers "a world of curses undergo" and they must return
"Into the good thoughts of the world again." They themselves remind Henry of the whole history of his exile; he retorts that by
complaints "Proclaim'd at market crosses, read in churches" they
have aroused the "fickle changelings and poor discontents" of the
whole land.

This swarming social and national life is set in place and time.
Pilgrims going to Canterbury, traders riding to London, men of
Herefordshire fighting in Wales, the Scots discomfited at Holmedon,
combattants by sandy-bottomed and sedgy-banked Severn, armies
converging on Shrewsbury from the North or through Gloucestershire and the Midlands—all these insist on topographical reality.
Indeed, the central scene on the rebels' side, that which most reveals
them, is the Bangor meeting, with the map for the tripartite division
and the quarrel over the "monstrous cantle" and the course of the
Trent. Time presses as hard as does place on the attention; history-
plays, after all, much more than comedies or tragedies fix the mind
on the sequence of past, present, and future, and on the hour which
strikes for action. The time here is sometimes the past, of Henry's
accession and reign, sometimes the future, of expected misrule, sometimes the present, of planned council-meetings or purse-takings or
campaign-details. But it always keeps us in the world of urgent
events.

All this is history coming to life. Part of it is the theme of horsemanship, so incident to rapid messages and highway robbery and war
and chivalry. Messengers "come with speed," "Stain'd with the
variation of each soil," spurring "with winged haste." Blunt enters
"newlighted" from his mission; Falstaff calls for his horse at Gad's
Hill as urgently as Hotspur for his at Warkworth; Hal and Peto,
with thirty miles to ride ere dinner-time, take "To horse, to horse."
This equestrian vitality culminates, like the animal imagery, in the
"fiery Pegasus" lines (IV.i.109–10), and Hotspur's reply (IV.i.119–23).
Horsemanship is a symbol of chivalric prowess, which is a main
subject of the play. When Hal appears most splendid he is vaulting

on his horse; it is "hot horse to horse" that Hotspur yearns to encounter him. Falstaff's "charge of foot" marks his significantly un-
chivalric status, as well as being Hal's joke at his expense.

The style, not yet as profound as it was to become in the tragedies,
has yet a full, active charge of meaning. It is vigorous and flexible
in syntax, and given to rapid evolution of metaphor. It is mimetic
—it expresses and enacts its meanings; it is powerful and resonant
in sound. . . .

Falstaff

Falstaff's transcendent prestige is reflected in a vast literature, and
in such abundant reference as to occasion, in the *Shakespeare Allu-
sion-Book* index, the telling entry, "For the purpose of this Index
Falstaff is treated as a work." This eminence is not predictable
from the life-story of his remote original Sir John Oldcastle (c. 1378–
1417), High Sheriff of Herefordshire, who became Lord Cobham by
marriage in 1409. Sir John steps into Holinshed in a role as remote
as can be imagined from the reverend vice and vanity in years; he
does not appear, moreover, until after the new-crowned Henry has
banished his youthful mates. "A valiant capteine and a hardie
gentleman" in the French wars, he has been "highly in the king's
favour" (Hol., iii.62), but is charged with Wycliffite heresy and con-
demned. Escaping from the Tower he hides in Wales, while his
supporters are cruelly suppressed, but eventually he is captured and
on Christmas Day 1417 is hanged and burnt.

The valiant Lollard could hardly have expected reincarnation as
Oldcastle-Falstaff. Falstaff's Biblical quotations might just possibly
reflect such antecedents; moreover, Oldcastle was cast off by the
King after early favour (some traditions date the rejection before,
some after, the accession); and during his trial he confessed

> that in my frayle youthe I offended thee (Lorde) moste greeuously, in
> Pride, Wrathe, and Glottony, in Couetousnes and in Lechery.[17]

But the resemblance is not strong. Oldcastle's posthumous story ran
in two contrasting channels.[18] One, hostile to him, is that of anti-
Wycliffite orthodoxy, and is found in the poet Hoccleve,[19] in popu-

---

[17] John Foxe, *Actes and Monuments*, 1563, 266.
[18] Thoroughly plotted by Wilhelm Baeske, *Oldcastle-Falstaff in der engl.
Literatur bis Sh.*, 1905.
[19] Hoccleve, *Works. I. The Minor Poems* (EETS, Extra ser., lxi, 1892, 8–24,
"Address to Sir John Oldcastle").

lar political verses, and in chroniclers from Walsingham to Poly-
dore Vergil. Fuller, it will be recalled, blamed "the *Papists* railing
on him for a *Heretick*" as the fabricators of his disrepute as a
coward. His flight to Wales and consequent absence from Henry's
later wars were misconstrued as pusillanimity; his Lollardism was
taken for presumption, blasphemy, and even diabolical instigation;
his friendship with the King was restricted to Henry's unregenerate
youth; and from his name he was wrongly assumed to be old. The
contrasting, favourable, tradition emerged with Tudor Protestant-
ism and is traceable to John Bale's *Brefe Chronycle Concernynge
. . . Syr Iohn Oldecastell* (1544). This influenced Hall and was reprinted almost verbatim in Foxe's *Actes and Monuments,* later
editions of which contained a long "Defense of the Lord Cobham"
and furnished the historical materials for the Munday-Drayton-
Wilson-Hathaway play. By this tradition "this most constaunt seru-
ant of the lord and worthy knight Sir John Oldecastell, the Lorde
Cobham," [20] was a Protestant hero and martyr, "a principall fa-
uourer, receiuer, and maintainer of . . . Lollards," [21] a scholar of
philosophy and theology, a popular and virtuous leader, wild when
young but a religious convert—"his youth was full of wanton wild-
ness before he knew the scriptures," says Bale—and not rejected
by Henry until some time after the coronation. Bale, however,
mistakenly endorsed the error about his age. These, then, are the
conflicting stories, germs of Oldcastle the vicious reprobate and Oldcastle the virtuous martyr, the former incorporated in *The Famous
Victories* and Shakespeare, the latter in *Sir John Oldcastle's* hero—

> It is no pampered glutton we present,
> Nor aged Councellor to youthfull sinne,
> But one, whose vertue shone aboue the rest,
> A valiant Martyr and a vertuous peere.

How Oldcastle came to be involved in stories of youthful riot is
a matter of speculation. The syllogism may have been that the
companions of the young Henry were scapegraces; that Oldcastle
was a companion of the young Henry; and that therefore Oldcastle
was a scapegrace. Professor Dover Wilson suggests that his rejection
by Henry welded itself in the popular mind with that of the scapegraces, the more readily since according to the hostile tradition
both occurred approximately at Henry's accession ("Before the
Kings coronacion [Oldcastle] was forsaken of the Kinge," says Tito

[20] John Foxe, *Actes and Monuments,* 1563, 263.
[21] Ibid., 1596 edn., i.513.

Livio's translator[22]) and the "confession" reported by Foxe might
be an effective link.

Since the historical Oldcastle was certainly neither old nor un-
military and (being a warrior) probably not fat, these attributes of
Falstaff must arise otherwise than from history. In fact, several
elements from the hostile tradition coalesced with features of the
popular morality Vice. Oldcastle's age (thirty-nine at death) was
exaggerated by the interpretation of his name on which Shakespeare puns in the "old lad of the castle"; but the Vice, too, was
often the aged counsellor to youthful sin. The shortage of valour is
derived from the hostile tradition, but it too was easily corroborated
by the pusillanimity of Vices, parasites, and boasters. The "goodly
portly" figure is in neither history nor *The Famous Victories,* and
attempts have been made to explain it. It may be Shakespeare's
dramatic contrast, Dover Wilson suggests, to that of the "starve-
ling" Prince (II.iv.240), whose lithe agility the chroniclers celebrate.
Or something may come from *Woodstock's* plump "old turkey-
cocke." But here again the Vice has something to contribute, as will
be seen.

Falstaff is indeed a rich amalgam, a world of comic ingredients.
Source-seekers have proffered his components in great profusion.
Of these the most important is the morality Vice, the ensnarer of
youth. Since Quiller-Couch proposed this in *Shakespeare's Work-
manship* (1918) the idea has been amply elaborated, and John W.
Shirley has excellently explored the relevant characteristics of
Gluttony, the Gula of the Seven Deadly Sins and a favourite
morality-play tempter.[23] Vices often bragged, like Sensual Appetyte,
or Ambidexter in *Cambises* (1569), or Lust, Sturdiness, and Inclina-
tion in *The Trial of Treasure.* They might sanctimoniously cham-

---

[22] Cf. C. L. Kingsford, *The First English Life of Henry V,* 1911, 22.

[23] "Fal. an Elizabethan Glutton" (*PQ,* xvii, 1938). In *The Castell of Perseverance*
(c. 1425), the World, Devil, and Flesh lead Mankind "with synnys al a-bowt";
Flesh is corpulent and accompanied by Gluttony, Lechery, and Sloth. In Med-
wall's *Nature* (c. 1486), aged Sensuality has Gluttony as an accomplice. In *The
Nature of the Foure Elements* (1519), Sensual Appetite under the guise of Friendship tempts Humanyte to the tavern, and in *Lusty Juventus* (c. 1540) the age-old
Hypocrisy incites Juventus to lechery and self-indulgence. In William Wager's
The Longer Thou Livest the More Fool Thou Art (c. 1586), Incontinence is
as old as Idleness, "parent of all vice," and tempts Man with food, wine, and
girls: in Lupton's *All for Money* (1578), Pleasure is glutton and lecher, and
Gluttony prompts to "fine fare and gluttonie." Ryot, in *Youth* (c. 1550), is
thief and tempter to wine and women; *The Trial of Treasure* (1567) has one
Gredy-Gutte—"the cowe-bellied knaue," "the great-bellied loute." In *The Faerie
Queene* (I.iv.21–23) Spenser's Gluttony is, like Falstaff, "Not meet to be of counsell
to a king," "Full of diseases," his belly "up-blowne with luxury."

pion virtue; "Uertue is mocked of euery man," laments Incontinence in *The Longer Thou Livest*. Collectively they share their features with the farce-clowns like Huanebango the braggart of Peele's *Old Wives' Tale*, or the greedy cowardly Dericke of *The Famous Victories*, whom Falstaff copies in making his nose bleed with speargrass (*1H4*, II.iv.305). An Elizabethan audience would recognize in Falstaff the familiar Vice-qualities of gluttony, idleness, and lechery, and in Hal the youth in danger. Throughout Falstaff is referred to in morality-idiom—iniquity, ruffian, vanity in years, beating Hal out of his kingdom with a dagger of lath, the abominable misleader of youth, the old white-bearded Satan; and in Part Two he is rejected finally (as prospectively in Part One, by Hal's soliloquy and many a hint) as the tutor and feeder of Hal's "riots" (a recognized morality-term), the old profane surfeit-swelled gormandizer. Hal's soliloquy (*1H4*, I.ii.190 ff.) tells the audience both that Hal is not the hooligan of *The Famous Victories* (which, incidentally, is not at all morality-influenced) and that he participates undeceived in the unyoked humours of idleness.

"Morality tradition" is a broad category. The various kinds of Vice-farce, with such conceits as clownage keeps in pay, furnish a wide panorama of aged, obese, gluttonous, wenching braggarts, comically outrageous in huffing, puffing, lying, thieving, and gormandizing. Somewhere in the picture are the *miles gloriosus*, with his bogus valour, and the witty parasite (both frequent in Plautine comedy), the fool, and the Elizabethan army officer often castigated for recruiting and other swindles. Enthusiasts have even sought Falstaff in historical persons—Tarlton the clown, Chettle the dramatist, and Captain Nicholas Dawtrey. Neglecting these agreeable whimsies we may admit something, though with reserve, in the other identifications. The *miles gloriosus* boasted of courage but avoided combat, like Bobadill in *Every Man in his Humour* or Parolles in *All's Well*, and scholars have worked out his contribution to Falstaff. Yet since he was fatuous, humourless, and finally unmasked to derision we may agree with Maurice Morgann that elements of the *miles gloriosus* in Falstaff are so modified by wit and self-possession as to become something different, a mere trace of flavour in a succulent gallimaufry, like the *soupçon* of Basilisco in the soliloquy on honour.

As for the parasite tradition, this contributed something; Iago has been called the culmination of the fatal parasite, Falstaff of the comic.[24] Butt, wit, sponger, trickster, and mocker, this classical type

---

[24] E. P. Vandiver, "The Elizabethan Dramatic Parasite," *SP*, 1935, xxxii. 411.

was familiar to the Elizabethan stage in such figures as Mathew
Merygreke in *Ralph Roister Doister* or Cariosophus in *Damon and
Pithias*. But again the relationship to Falstaff is only tangential;
Falstaff is a parasite but a benefactor too, and much else besides.

His quality as Fool, however, is more noteworthy, for he shares
not only some of the Fool's superficial features—comic braggadocio,
inventiveness of idea, dexterity with words, mock moralizing, deliberate mistakings, absurd actions—but also the Fool's deeper significance, as liberator from convention. In Miss Enid Welsford's
words:

> under the dissolvent influence of [the Fool's] personality the iron net-
> work of physical, social, and moral law, which enmeshes us from the
> cradle to the grave, seems—for the moment—negligible as a web of
> gossamer. The Fool does not lead a revolt against the law; he lures
> us into a region of the spirit where, as Lamb would put it, the writ
> does not run.   (*The Fool*, 1935, 317)

We cannot always live in that region, as the play makes clear, nor
is its freedom, as some Falstaff sentimentalists suggest, more precious than the network of law. But Miss Welsford does in fact
admirably describe the effect Falstaff has upon our spirits.[25]

Falstaff as a whole is far greater than the sum of his parts; this
Vice–Parasite–Fool–*Miles-Gloriosus*–Corrupt-Soldier is inspired by
such humorous virtuosity as immeasurably to transcend such components. His whole nature is unified of paradoxical opposites, so
that a man no more knows where to have him than he himself
knew where to have the Hostess (III.iii.126–27). Parasitical, he yet
gives to life as much as he takes, and indeed provides amidst all his
vices a vast salutary criticism of the world of war and policy. He is
vicious, yet his vices are a tonic for human nature; he exploits his
dependants, yet they remain indissolubly attached to him; he lies,
yet would be dismayed if his lies were to be believed. He laments
his age, corpulence, and lost agility, yet he behaves with the gaiety
of youth, has intellectual legerity to offset his bulk, and is agile
whenever it suits him. A reprobate, he yet quotes scripture for his
purpose. Finally, is he or is he not a coward? No, say Morgann and
Bradley: he is sought for in war, leads his men into danger, and
philosophizes coolly on the battlefield. Yes, say Stoll and others: as
Poins foretells, he runs at Gad's Hill and boasts afterwards; he

---

[25] Cf. C. L. Barber, "From Ritual to Comedy," 24, in *English Stage Comedy*,
ed. W. K. Wimsatt, 1955: "In the theatrical institution of clowning, the clown
or vice, when Shakespeare started to write, was a recognized anarchist who made
aberration obvious by carrying release to absurd extremes."

hacks his sword, slubbers his garments, and is touchy when taunted; his Shrewsbury nonchalance is clown-foolery only; his ignominious stabbing of Hotspur is "one of the accepted *lazzi* of the coward on the stage"; and his capture of Colevile in Part Two is buffoonery, like Pistol's of Monsieur le Fer in *Henry V*.

This tiresome question need not have arisen had not Morgann rightly desired to vindicate Falstaff from the ignominious clowning he received on the eighteenth-century stage. It would have been quickly settled had not Falstaff's vitality confused critics as to the difference between dramatic and real persons. This multifarious material is not to be reduced to a single realistic formula. That Falstaff's panic at Gad's Hill is not put on there is no doubt. It is a foretold outcome of the trick played on him; the point of "By the Lord, I knew ye as well as he that made ye" (II.iv.263) is to show his resourcefulness in improbable excuse; and the surprised relief in "But by the Lord, lads, I am glad you have the money" (II.iv.271–72) is proof that he had thought the booty to be lost. The multiplication of buckram men does not mean either on the one hand that he expects to be believed or on the other that he has recognized his assailants and is pulling their legs: he is putting on the expected enjoyable show. And who, in fact, is "he"? "He," really, is the comic personality given a chance by the dramatist to revel in a comic role. The exaggerations are not to be explained realistically by the argument that so acute a wit cannot expect so absurd a yarn to be believed and is merely countermining the Prince and Poins for the trick he has detected: he has not detected it, but, like the brilliant stage-comic he is, he has an invention full of nimble and delectable shapes which he exercises on all possible occasions with the effect (eagerly expected by Prince, Poins, and audience alike) of landing himself in foreseeable quandaries and then unforeseeably extricating himself from them.[26] To schematize Falstaff's shotsilk variety into stable colour is absurd: his dramatic sphere of popular comedy allows a rapid shifting of attitudes. A real man who ran at Gad's Hill would not receive a charge of foot from his stampeder, nor would a dozen captains seek him out, nor even with Hal's connivance would anyone believe he had killed Hotspur. But the stage comic frees us from the restricting congruities of real life. Professor Empson has put it (it is Dover Wilson's plea too) that "the whole of the great joke is that you *can't* see through him, any more than the Prince could"—"the dramatic effect simply *is* the doubt, and very

[26] A. J. A. Waldock comments well to this effect in "The Men in Buckram," *RES*, 1947, XXIII, 16–23.

satisfying too." [27] Is Falstaff then inconsistent? Yes, if judged realistically. No, when taken, rightly, for what Empson calls his "Dramatic Ambiguity," for the figure of dramatic comedy that he is, butt and wit together, equally amusing by his elephantine panic, exuberant fabrications, and comic aplomb in the midst of war. His philosophy of courage is, no doubt, to show as much or as little of it as circumstances require; he might observe, like the practical but not cowardly Bluntschli in Shaw's *Arms and the Man,* "It is our duty to live as long as we can," and like Bluntschli he keeps in his holster something better than pistols. Yet Bluntschli would hardly "roar" in flight, as Falstaff does (II.ii.106), and the attempt to fit Falstaff into a formula of psychological realism must finally fail. Brilliant at timely evasions, he escapes this straitjacket as he escapes any other.

In other words, Falstaff, though immensely "living," is not like any single real man. But he is symbolically like life itself; the large comedy of humanity is embodied in him. He expresses the indispensable spirit of fun. When he runs away, the fun is at him; when he does not run away, the fun is through him. The consistency lies not in the congruence of one action with another, but in the whole function of providing mirth and a liberating irreverence. Falstaff differs in amplitude but not in kind from the stage funny man who, without incongruity, is both knocked about and knocker-about. In the words Whitman wrote on himself, he is large, he contains multitudes.

[27] W. Empson, "Fal. and Mr. Dover Wilson," *Kenyon Review,* 1953, XV, 223.

Ceremony and History: The Problem of Symbol from *Richard II* to *Henry V*

by Eric La Guardia

Ceremony and history are the terms I have chosen to identify the clash of divinity and mortality, and to suggest a way of dealing with the problem of symbol in the plays. The distinction between the two terms is similar to the distinction made by Sidney between golden and brazen worlds. The word "history" is meant to indicate event itself; the unselected and even chaotic flow of actuality. The historical world is a world of contingency, objective fact, and temporality. Brazen nature, in Sidney's usage, has the same meaning. It is restricted to the existential, while the golden world of poetry imitates that which ought to be—growing "in effect into another nature." The creation of a second nature, the departure from perceived actuality, mimetic reality, a formalized mode of existence—these are the characteristics of "ceremony" and the ceremonious world. The leap from the golden world, whose meaning has been poetically granted, to the world of the ceremonious should not be too difficult, for the world of majesterial ceremonies is a condition of experience which takes its meaning only from the sacred symbolic forms by which it functions. Ceremony takes a sacramental view of nature; it operates within mythical rather than historical time; it attempts to preserve the order of culture in opposition to the disorderly flow of human experience.

It is important to keep in mind that ceremony and history are continually interacting. This counterpoint between the two worlds makes a final judgment of their relative value impossible. It is by no means implausible to argue that the narrative movement from

From "*Ceremony and History: The Problem of Symbol from Richard II to Henry V*," by Eric La Guardia. From Pacific Coast Studies in Shakespeare, ed. W. F. McNeir and T. N. Greenfield (Eugene, Oregon: University of Oregon Books, 1966), pp. 70–72, 78–82, 85–88. Copyright © 1966 University of Oregon. Reprinted by permission of the publisher.

the mystical kingship of Richard to the rational kingship of Henry V is a healthy destruction of the mythical character of the state, superseded by a vital acceptance of the immediate historical moment. Yet, it is also possible to interpret the same movement as the destruction of a divinely sanctioned culture, superseded by detachment, cunning, and political expediency. We may claim that the plays dramatize the emergence of a culture purged of the nonhistorical formalism of Christian chivalry into a brighter world where the autonomous reality of nature is recognized. Or, we may claim that they dramatize the tragic death of the sacramental view of nature, together with its kindred poetic sensibility, and the rise of a new order of anarchy, libertinism, and political opportunism.

The conflict of claims is resolved if we see that both narrative movements proceed simultaneously in a subtle dramatic organization. The plays dramatize the dehumanization of culture caused by the vanities of sacred symbolic forms and the secularization of the divine order of culture caused by the new emphasis upon immediate, nonsymbolic experience. The effect of this counterpoint is to establish an ironic relationship between divinity and mortality, a relationship in which the profane is made sacred, the sacred profane. The extravagance of Richard's poetic sensibility suggests at the outset a decadence inherent in the chivalric, formal modes of existence so that it recommends itself to purgation and replacement by a new order. Yet, we can not be entirely confident in the profane existence of Prince Hal, or in Henry V's merely rhetorical commitment to the vestigial forms of sacred majesty which remain in the state. That the four plays trace the decline of symbolic order or forms is quite clear; but we are not asked to judge whether that decline is pure gain or pure loss. It would seem wiser to think of them as dramatizing man's continuous participation in both the mythical and historical.

The mimetic function of the king as God's vicar, manifested in all ceremonious procedures, provides the link required here to relate the theme of ceremony and history to the problem of symbol. The world in which the ceremonies of sacred majesty prevail is governed by an almost exclusive faith in the reality of symbolic forms. The bond between heaven and England is maintained symbolically, ritualistically, ceremoniously. And it is primarily through verbal behavior that the possibilities of symbolic forms in general are illuminated for us. Excessive faith in symbol or ceremony is represented by Richard II. At the other extreme stands Henry V, committed to history rather than ceremony. Between these extremes the drama of the possibilities of the symbolic forms of language takes place. The polarity which organizes this four-part drama is that of the symbolic and the actual, a revised and more sharply focused version of the polarity of ceremony and history. . . .

In the whole of *Richard II,* the consistency with which its immediate dramatic concerns take the form of the dualism of the expressed and the existential is discernible. The variety of motifs in the play is given structural unity by the preoccupation with the problem of symbology. The simplest statement of the basic conflict in the play is that there is a continual counterpoint of the equation of word and object, and the separation of word and object. Despite certain important revisions in his philosophy of language at the end of the play, Richard is the pre-eminent representative of the magical oneness of the symbolic and the objective. The tragic nature of "poetical man" is communicated to us through this character. And the picture of poetical man is extreme, for it consists of an excessive visceral response to the sublimity of trope, a belief in word-magic, the vanity of "poet-as-god," the confusion of mortality and divinity, and the primacy of ceremony over history. Serving as a foil to poetical man, generally speaking, is the figure of Bolingbroke, scornful of the shadow world of eloquence and "bare imagination." The play, however, is Richard's; and in spite of his tragic confusion of mortality and divinity, manifest in his tendency to consider symbolic forms substantial, we should not forget that he somehow manages at the end to transform the sublime trope into a vital tool for self-knowledge, by which he discovers his mortality.

The refraction of reality into deluding images is presumably no longer a characteristic of the two *Henry IV* plays. The symbolic forms of Richard's court no longer seem possible instruments of government or viable elements of consciousness. The fictional world of these two plays is one of greatly expanded awareness, a world peopled by vital characters as well as discontented thoughts. The narrative movement is forward into the immediacy of history, throwing into darkness the ceremonious world of absolutes. The sacred order is replaced by the natural, eliminating the sacramental and the animistic; and in turn devaluing the magical operation of symbols.

This ascendancy of nature or history over ceremony, however, is not a simple matter of the metamorphosis of the political state and the individual consciousness. The new historical reality is dramatized as not only a liberation of the immediate moment from the imposition of symbolic forms, but as an anarchy of manifold experiences as well. In addition, language retains its uncertain character as both disguising and revealing reality. Although a direct approach to historical experience, unmediated by language and leading to unequivocal and effective action, seems to be the personal and political goal of these plays, there is evident the continuing need of "forms" to bestow an order of meaning upon a world animated merely by the flow of time. Dramatically, the greatest share of the responsibility for reconciling experiences and forms falls to the young Prince, whose own personal equilibrium, like the state's, is at stake. While King Richard's crisis of consciousness called for the divestiture of a symbolic attitude hopelessly sacramental, the young Prince is required to reconstruct a symbolic order of monarchy out of the most diverse and unpromising materials: residues of the dying political theology of the king's two bodies; chivalric protocols of the court and battlefield; majesterial rhetoric; the prodigalities of the tavern, and Falstaffian wit and cynicism.

As a symbolic form, language is paradoxically employed in these plays to criticize the presumption of the symbolic itself. The prime agent in this ambiguous use of language is Falstaff, although the general characteristic of being suspicious of eloquence but indulging in it is evident in both Hotspur and the Prince. The Prince is Falstaff's detached but authentic disciple for some time, indulging in the same kind of linguistic extravagances. In addition, as Henry V he comes to an impressive understanding of the relationship between ceremony and history, according to which the language of majesty is moribund yet extremely effective in maintaining an ordered state. Poetical self-indulgence is replaced finally by the art of persuasive speech. And Hotspur, the apparent champion of action uncluttered by words, indulges in the excessive chivalric vocabulary of military honor and is accused of apprehending a "world of figures" in place of the actual. Each emphasis upon the insufficiency of words is balanced, as it were, by a counterstress on the power of words. The expansion of consciousness, the multiplicity of perceptions, the increase of knowledge represented by this new world, cannot exist without the formative function of language. The nameless and the speechless eliminate meaning. This particular point is in subtle contrast to the idea of the ground of reality conveyed through the metaphors of namelessness and nothingness in *Richard II*, both in the Queen's doctrine and in Richard's final conception of "nothing." [1]

---

[1] Recall, however, that Richard's conception of "nothing" also means death, suggesting the morbid result of devaluing words. Note also the association between silence and death in Mowbray's reaction to his banishment: "What is thy sentence then but speechless death" (I.iii.172); and Northumberland after the death of Gaunt: "His tongue is now a stringless instrument" (II.i.149).

The counterpoint of words and experience is matched by the counterpoint of ceremony and history. Whatever loss results from the rejection of ceremonious forms is precariously balanced by gains derived from the increased perception of the natural. On the other hand, this realization of the disorderly flow of history brings with it a new and somber attitude toward time in which the mutable and temporal become a burden to consciousness.[2] The death of the elaborate symbolic order of ceremonious majesty results in a newly abundant world of actuality; yet this world itself requires forms to rescue it from chaos. Henry IV, close to death, says bitterly and sardonically to the Prince, "mock at form/. . . Up vanity!/Down, royal state." The need for the state not to mock forms is also made clear in the rejection of Falstaff, "so surfeit-swelled, so old, and so profane"; and more explicitly by the newly crowned Henry V:

> The tide of blood in me
> Hath proudly flow'd in vanity till now:
> Now doth it turn and ebb back to the sea,
> Where it shall mingle with the state of floods
> And flow henceforth in formal majesty.
> (*2 Henry IV*, V.ii.129–33)

The problematic nature of the newly developed historical awareness and its connection with ceremony is largely revealed in the anarchy of language, a condition which necessitates the profanation of a sublime poetry, and the liberation of metaphor from the bondage of magical usage. The new valuation of language in which diverse symbolic potentials are simultaneously eliminated and released is most radically embodied in the figure of Falstaff, who serves to bring together both attitudes toward language—one scornful of words, the other bordering on the idolatrous:

> The brain of this foolish-compounded clay, man, is not able to invent anything that intends to laughter more than I invent or is invented on me. I am not only witty in myself, but the cause that wit is in other men. (*2 Henry IV*, I.ii.8–12)

Falstaff is not only the source and victim of all comic invention, but, more subtly, the creator of a new mode of language as well.

---

[2] In the despair and ineffectiveness of King Henry IV this burden of time is evident. For example: "So shaken as we are, so wan with care" (*1 Henry IV*, I.i.i); or, ". . . how chances mock,/And changes fill the cup of alteration/With divers liquors!" (*2 Henry IV*, III.i.51–53). In contrast to the oppression of time is the Prince's recognition of Falstaff's divorce from time: "What a devil hast thou to do with the time of the day?" (*1 Henry IV*, I.ii.6).

At best it eliminates the mystery of the word made flesh and the attendant vanities of language, replacing them with a commitment to abundant nature. At worst it degenerates into the doctrine of accommodation, according to which the abundance of nature is met with a corresponding abundance of words.[3]

It is impossible to miss the irony in Falstaff's victory over the mystery of incarnation. The *embodiment* of language is to him an absurd idea. His recognition of the separation between what is present in fact and what may be mimetically conveyed by the word is evident throughout his career. Sensual response to manifold nature is opposed to mere words. Yet his powers of mimesis and invention are incomparable—his apparently instinctive knowledge of stylistics, his capacity to "stand for" both the Prince and the King, the witty conjuration by which he multiplies the buckram men. In his massive corporeality, it would seem, the word resides. He becomes, by virtue of being the source of all invention, the ironic incarnation of the possibilities of language. His figure stands as a summation of the uncertain relationship between corporeality and metaphoric reality. The world of madcap linguistic forms over which he presides is his own symbolic creation. He generates its forms, and is in turn recipient of them. In this particular characteristic, we cannot fail to see Falstaff's ironic association with Richard II. Although the two figures seem poles apart because of their mutually exclusive commitments to the historical and to the ceremonious, an extraordinary presumption of language gives them a strange kinship. In both cases the belief in the power of the word supersedes almost all other considerations. For Richard it is the only satisfactory means of participating in the mystery of kingship. For Falstaff it is a secular form of populating the world with the particles of his wit, an ironic function of godhood.

In the witty union of gross body and creative power, we recognize both the success and the failure of Falstaff's new mode of language. He exists, that is, both historically and ceremoniously. His sensuality is matched by his own particular kind of eloquence, profane in its content, but symbolic by virtue of its power to vitiate the contingency of profane actuality itself. That he is aware of the difference between the metaphorical and the real is clear from his running critique of a wide variety of symbolic forms, and from his mounting apprehension over the absolute surety of rejection by the king. Although Henry's artfully created state cannot operate in

---

[3] The doctrine of accommodation (see *2 Henry IV*, I.ii.276–78; III.ii.–72–87) points toward the expedient rhetoric of Henry V, and ultimately to the brilliant Machiavellian performance of Richard III.

terms of Falstaff's symbolic forms, it is impossible not to feel the effects of a further decline of creative power in his rejection of those forms. Perhaps the loss here is even greater than in *Richard II,* for in Falstaff an acute consciousness of the objective, historical world is combined with a successful verbal expression of that world. His doom seems to come, however, not only from the hard requirements of statecraft, but also from the absurdities and commodities of the tavern, an excess reflected in the overexpansion of the possibilities of language. Even at the moment of his death Falstaff is far from silent, if we are to believe the Hostess. He may even have created in his fancy an extravagant poetic image of Arcadian fields. . . .

In these history plays Shakespeare dramatizes a continuously uneasy equilibrium between the creative power of the imagination (which at its furthest limit tends to atrophy the will) and the abundance of immediate experience (which at its furthest limit tends to demolish the continuity of forms created by the imagination). There is no doubt that a political community has come to be more efficiently organized with the victory of history over ceremony under Henry V; but it is equally clear that Shakespeare has given a Pyrrhic quality to this victory.

Throughout these four plays there is a crucial relationship between consciousness and the use of language. We begin with the narrow, private consciousness of the arch-poet for whom the sublime trope is abundantly concrete. Is this not to be applauded, the creative power of the poet to turn the word to flesh? It is clear that, for Shakespeare, Richard has done something wrong. His conception of poetry is not dramatized as viable, although at the end we do observe Richard's tormented but largely victorious struggle with the possibilities of metaphor. One of his errors is presumption—the mythical embodiment of the word must not be taken too literally, at least if one is mortal. Also, Richard seems to have a reversed concept of metaphor, so that an object becomes virtually a symbol for its word. Nature itself becomes expressive, rather than language. Thus, in spite of the seemingly pure equation of word and object, Richard's perversion of symbol is made clear.

The decadence, however, is not without implications of value. We can sense the virtue of the poet-king, perhaps, only when the consciousness of the last king is understood. His knowledge of the analogical relationship between forms and experiences is complete and rational. This means that he knows just how uncertain the nature of symbol is. The precarious connection between language and being resides in the very requirement of granting meaning to existence through symbolic forms, the necessity of generating analogical and mediatory relationships between different "orders" of reality. It is the problematic nature of metaphor itself, by means of which an imitation of reality is undertaken that may result in either the illumination or the benighting of truth. Symbolic forms provide us with our "given world," yet the ontological status of those forms is always in question.

The counterpoint of the real and the symbolic suggests that the governing idea in these plays is symbology, taking that term to mean the possibilities of imagery in relation to the contingencies of experience. Mimesis is a theme, not only a technique. In this theme, the presented and the represented are in search of equilibrium. The reliance upon mimetic precedures, the formalism of chivalry, is singularly strong in the first king. This kind of indulgence is revaluated during the reign of Falstaff, and again by the last king, who secularizes the mystery of the creative power of the king as god and poet (but in whom is evident the continuation of the idea of the state as a work of art). The drama of the decline of poetical man and the rise of rhetorical man is also the drama of the collectivization of language. Richard is punished for his private and ultimately nonpolitical use of eloquence. Too personal and magical, it would seem, for the maintenance of an intelligible state. Words devoted impersonally to ordering the state by means of the collective function of rhetoric rise in the place of poetry.

Flesh and word are in constant opposition, threatening each other's autonomy. The order of words is destroyed under the abundant weight of the concrete. And, the artifice of language may dehumanize the expansive world of the human will. This continual confrontation, clash, and revaluation of forms and experience is descriptive of both a problem of poetry and a problem of culture. The symbolic act of naming bestows a pattern of meaning upon the flow of history, thereby transforming it into a culture. The continuity of the tradition is in continual danger of destruction through insistent revaluations by immediate moments of experience (which ironically take their place, eventually, as items of tradition); and, conversely, the heavy imposition of the absolutes of inherited culture is always threatening to eliminate the manifold, novel possibilities of these immediate moments. The perpetual tension between the order of words and the order of nature is presumably necessary for the dynamic renewal of history. The character of this tension raises a persistent question: Are the symbolic forms of culture the only true index of reality, or are they a distortion of reality? Are the meanings granted to existence by language insidious configurations or not?

Shakespeare raises, explores, and illuminates the question. In these plays the culture of the Middle Ages is represented as partially transmitted and partially annihilated. The emergent culture lays claim to the importance of immediacy, contingency, and expediency; yet it struggles with residues of the older world, and is often either incapable of or ineffective in creating its own metaphors of order. The medieval chivalric world provided Shakespeare with a vast culture-paradigm for the idea of "symbolic form" itself. It is dramatically employed as a great symbol for the very nature of symbol. Its multiplicity of formalities serves as a starting point for an inquiry into the question of the place occupied by "form" in human existence. The drama of culture is, in terms of a crisis of breakdown and revaluation, the eternal confrontation of history with its ceremonious past.

An historical dynamic emerges from Shakespeare's presentation of this dualism between the sacred design of tradition and the manifold possibilities of immediate experience. In this poeticized dynamic, the desire for deliverance from the burden of nature through symbolic forms is in continuous conflict with the inescapable sensation of the value of actuality itself. If the ceremonious is capable of victory over the historical (nature), such human presumption may lead to tragic consequences. On the other hand, if the historical totally eliminates the ceremonious, there can be no redemption from the anarchy of time. Such uncertainty seems to remain as a necessary aspect of the historical view imitated in the plays. The symbolic, the ceremonious, and the poetic may constitute a deliverance from nature by virtue of their creative power to grant order. Or they may set up destructive and tragic mediations between man and truth.

This reciprocal but problematic relationship between word and experience may be perceived as a dramatization of poetry itself, as well as a dramatization of man caught between the counterclaims of ceremony and history. The problem of symbol, which is at the center of these plays, is given dramatic shape by confronting the value of a poetic order of words with the value of the multiple and unlimited possibilities of existence itself. A world shaped by art and thereby transformed into a culture comes to represent the whole idea of symbol. And the power of symbol to grant meaning to existence encounters, seemingly at the very moment when it operates as an ideal form of order, the retaliation of the opposite force of nature. A characteristic resolution of this tension in the Renaissance is to give to art some of the qualities of nature, and to give to nature some of the qualities of art. This metaphorical answer to the problem of symbol does not occur in these four plays. They illuminate, rather, the permanent struggle which results from the confrontation of symbolic design and objective world, a struggle to liberate the self from art. It is ironic that a prime requirement of this struggle is the failure to accomplish such a liberation, for the created world of forms is necessary for the imitation of this profound meeting of the individual and the ideology of art.

Rule and Misrule in *Henry IV*

by C. L. Barber

If all the year were playing holidays,
To sport would be as tedious as to work . . .

The two parts of *Henry IV*, written probably in 1597 and 1598,
are an astonishing development of drama in the direction of in-
clusiveness, a development possible because of the range of the
traditional culture and the popular theater, but realized only because Shakespeare's genius for construction matched his receptivity.
We . . . noticed briefly in the introductory chapter how, early in
his career, Shakespeare made brilliant use of the long standing
tradition of comic accompaniment and counterstatement by the
clown.[1] Now suddenly he takes the diverse elements in the pot-
pourri of the popular chronicle play and composes a structure in
which they draw each other out. The Falstaff comedy, far from
being forced into an alien environment of historical drama, is be-
gotten by that environment, giving and taking meaning as it grows.
The implications of the saturnalian attitude are more drastically
and inclusively expressed here than anywhere else, because here
misrule is presented along with rule and along with the tensions
that challenge rule. Shakespeare dramatizes not only holiday but
also the need for holiday and the need to limit holiday.

It is in the Henry IV plays that we can consider most fruitfully
general questions concerning the relation of comedy to analogous
forms of symbolic action in folk rituals: not only the likenesses of
comedy to ritual, but the differences, the features of comic form

From "Rule and Misrule in Henry IV," by C. L. Barber. From Shakespeare's
Festive Comedy *(Princeton, N.J.: Princeton University Press, 1959), pp. 192–213.
Originally published as "From Ritual to Comedy: An Examination of Henry IV"
in* English Stage Comedy, *ed. W. K. Wimsatt, Jr. (New York, 1955). Reprinted by
permission of AMS Press, Inc.*

[1] See [Barber, *Shakespeare's Festive Comedy*], pp. 12–13.

which make it comedy and not ritual. Such analogies, I think, prove to be useful critical tools: they lead us to see structure in the drama. And they also raise fascinating historical and theoretical questions about the relation of drama to other products of culture. One way in which our time has been seeing the universal in literature has been to find in complex literary works patterns which are analogous to myths and rituals and which can be regarded as archetypes, in some sense primitive or fundamental. I have found this approach very exciting indeed. But at the same time, such analysis can be misleading if it results in equating the literary form with primitive analogues. When we are dealing with so developed an art as Shakespeare's, in so complex an epoch as the Renaissance, primitive patterns may be seen in literature mainly because literary imagination, exploiting the heritage of literary form, disengages them from the suggestions of a complex culture. And the primitive levels are articulated in the course of reunderstanding their nature —indeed, the primitive can be fully expressed only on condition that the artist can deal with it in a most civilized way. Shakespeare presents patterns analogous to magic and ritual in the process of redefining magic as imagination, ritual as social action.

Shakespeare was the opposite of primitivistic, for in his culture what we search out and call primitive was in the blood and bone as a matter of course; the problem was to deal with it, to master it. The Renaissance, moreover, was a moment when educated men were modifying a ceremonial conception of human life to create a historical conception. The ceremonial view, which assumed that names and meanings are fixed and final, expressed experience as pageant and ritual—pageant where the right names could march in proper order, or ritual where names could be changed in the right, the proper way. The historical view expresses life as drama. People in drama are not identical with their names, for they gain and lose their names, their status and meaning—and not by settled ritual: the gaining and losing of names, of meaning, is beyond the control of any set ritual sequence. Shakespeare's plays are full of pageantry and of action patterned in a ritualistic way. But the pageants are regularly interrupted; the rituals are abortive or perverted; or if they succeed, they succeed against odds or in an unexpected fashion. The people in the plays try to organize their lives by pageant and ritual, but the plays are dramatic precisely because the effort fails. This failure drama presents as history and personality; in the largest perspective, as destiny.

At the heart of the plays there is, I think, a fascination with the individualistic use or abuse of ritual—with magic. There is an intoxication with the possibility of an omnipotence of mind by which words might become things, by which a man might "gain a deity," might achieve, by making his own ritual, an unlimited power to incarnate meaning.[2] This fascination is expressed in the poetry by which Shakespeare's people envisage their ideal selves. But his drama also expresses an equal and complementary awareness that magic is delusory, that words can become things or lead to deeds only within a social group, by virtue of a historical, social situation beyond the mind and discourse of any one man. This awareness of limitations is expressed by the ironies, whether comic or tragic, which Shakespeare embodies in the dramatic situations of his speakers, the ironies which bring down the meanings which fly high in winged words.

In using an analogy with temporary king and scapegoat to bring out patterns of symbolic action in Falstaff's role, it will be important to keep it clear that the analogy is one we make now, that it is not Shakespeare's analogy; otherwise we falsify his relation to tradition.[3] He did not need to discriminate consciously, in our way,

[2] Fascination with the abuse of ritual is nowhere clearer than in Marlowe's *Tamburlaine* and *Dr. Faustus.*

[3] The use of analogies like the scapegoat rituals can be misleading, or merely amusing, if the pattern is not rigorously related to the imaginative process in the play. Janet Spens, a student of Gilbert Murray's, wrote in 1916 a brief study which attempted to establish the presence of ritual patterns in Shakespeare's work (*An Essay on Shakespeare's Relation to Tradition,* Oxford, 1916). She throws out some brilliant suggestions. But her method for the most part consists of leaping intuitively from folklore to the plots of the plays, via the hypothesis of lost intermediary folk plays; and the plots, abstracted from the concrete emphasis of their dramatic realization, can be adjusted to square with an almost unlimited range of analogies. Miss Spens argues, for example, that because Antonio in *The Merchant of Venice* is enigmatically detached from personal concerns, and because in accepting the prospect of death at Shylock's hands he says, "I am the tainted wether of the flock," he "is" the Scapegoat. To be sure, at a very general level there is a partial analogy to scapegoat rituals, since Antonio is undertaking to bear the consequence of Bassanio's extravagance; and perhaps the pound of flesh motif goes back ultimately, through the tangle of legend and story tradition, to some such ceremonial. But there is no controlling such analogies if we go after them by catching at fragments of narrative; and one can understand, on that basis, the impulse to give up the whole approach as hopelessly capricious.

The case is altered, however, if attention is focused, not on this or that group of people in this or that story, but on the roles the persons are given in the play. When we are concerned to describe dramatic form—the rhythm of feeling and awareness in the audience which is focused through complementary roles in the fable and implemented by concrete patterns of language and gesture—then the form of rituals is relevant to the form of the plays as a parallel expression of the same kind of organization of experience.

underlying configurations which came to him with his themes and
materials. His way of extending consciousness of such patterns was
the drama. In creating the Falstaff comedy, he fused two main
saturnalian traditions, the clowning customary on the stage and
the folly customary on holiday, and produced something unprece-
dented. He was working out attitudes towards chivalry, the state
and crown in history, in response to the challenge posed by the
fate he had dramatized in *Richard II*. The fact that we find analogies to the ritual interregnum relevant to what Shakespeare produced is not the consequence of a direct influence; his power of
dramatic statement, in developing saturnalian comedy, reached to
modes of organizing experience which primitive cultures have developed with a clarity of outline comparable to that of his drama.
The large and profound relations he expressed were developed
from the relatively simple dramatic method of composing with
statement and counterstatement, elevated action and burlesque. The
Henry IV plays are masterpieces of the popular theater whose plays
were, in Sidney's words, "neither right tragedies nor right comedies,
mingling kings and clowns."

Mingling Kings and Clowns

The fascination of Falstaff as a dramatic figure has led criticism,
from Morgann's essay onward, to center *1 Henry IV* on him, and
to treat the rest of the play merely as a setting for him. But despite
his predominating imaginative significance, the play is centered on
Prince Hal, developing in such a way as to exhibit in the prince an
inclusive, sovereign nature fitted for kingship. The relation of the
Prince to Falstaff can be summarized fairly adequately in terms of
the relation of holiday to everyday. As the non-historical material
came to Shakespeare in *The Famous Victories of Henry the Fifth,*
the prince was cast in the traditional role of the prodigal son, while
his disreputable companions functioned as tempters in the same
general fashion as the Vice of the morality plays. At one level
Shakespeare keeps this pattern, but he shifts the emphasis away
from simple moral terms. The issue, in his hands, is not whether
Hal will be good or bad but whether he will be noble or degener-
ate, whether his holiday will become his everyday. The interregnum
of a Lord of Misrule, delightful in its moment, might develop
into the anarchic reign of a favorite dominating a dissolute king.
Hal's secret, which he confides early to the audience, is that for
him Falstaff is merely a pastime, to be dismissed in due course:

> If all the year were playing holidays,
> To sport would be as tedious as to work;
> But when they seldom come, they wish'd-for come . . .
>
> (I.ii.228–30)

The prince's sports, accordingly, express not dissoluteness but a fine excess of vitality—"as full of spirit as the month of May"—together with a capacity for occasionally looking at the world as though it were upside down. His energy is controlled by an inclusive awareness of the rhythm in which he is living: despite appearances, he will not make the mistake which undid Richard II, who played at saturnalia until it caught up with him in earnest. During the battle of Shrewsbury (when, in Hotspur's phrase, "Doomsday is near"), Hal dismisses Falstaff with "What! is it a time to jest and dally now?" (V.iii.57) This sense of timing, of the relation of holiday to everyday and doomsday, contributes to establishing the prince as a sovereign nature.

But the way Hal sees the relations is not the way other people see them, nor indeed the way the audience sees them until the end. The holiday-everyday antithesis is his resource for control, and in the end he makes it stick. But before that, the only clear-cut definition of relations in these terms is in his single soliloquy, after his first appearance with Falstaff. Indeed, it is remarkable how little satisfactory formulation there is of the relationships which the play explores dramatically. It is essential to the play that the prince should be misconstrued, that the king should see "riot and dishonor stain" (I.i.85) his brow, that Percy should patronize him as a "nimble-footed madcap" (IV.ii.95) who might easily be poisoned with a pot of ale if it were worth the trouble. But the absence of adequate summary also reflects the fact that Shakespeare was doing something which he could not summarize, which only the whole resources of his dramatic art could convey.

It is an open question, throughout *Part One,* as to just who or what Falstaff is. At the very end, when Prince John observes "This is the strangest tale that ever I heard," Hal responds with "This is the strangest fellow, brother John" (V.iv.158–59). From the beginning, Falstaff is constantly renaming himself:

> Marry, then, sweet wag, when thou art king, let not us that are squires of the night's body be called thieves of the day's beauty. Let us be Diana's Foresters, Gentlemen of the Shade, Minions of the Moon; and let men say we be men of good government. . . .   (I.ii.26–31)

Here Misrule is asking to be called Good Government, as it is his role to do—though he does so with a wink which sets real good government at naught, concluding with "steal":

> . . . men of good government, being governed as the sea is, by our noble and chaste mistress the moon, under whose countenance we steal.
> (I.ii.31–33)

I have considered in an earlier chapter how the witty equivocation Falstaff practices, like that of Nashe's Bacchus and other apologists for folly and vice, alludes to the very morality it is flouting. Such "damnable iteration" is a sport that implies a rolling-eyed awareness of both sides of the moral medal; the Prince summarizes it in saying that Sir John "was never yet a breaker of proverbs. He will give the devil his due" (I.ii.131–33). It is also a game to be played with cards close to the chest. A Lord of Misrule naturally does not call himself Lord of Misrule in setting out to reign, but takes some title with the life of pretense in it. Falstaff's pretensions, moreover, are not limited to one occasion, for he is not properly a holiday lord, but a *de facto* buffoon who makes his way by continually seizing, catch as catch can, on what names and meanings the moment offers. He is not a professed buffoon—few buffoons, in life, are apt to be. In Renaissance courts, the role of buffoon was recognized but not necessarily formalized, not necessarily altogether distinct from the role of favorite. And he is a highwayman: Shakespeare draws on the euphemistic, mock-chivalric cant by which "the profession" grace themselves. Falstaff in *Part One* plays it that he is Hal's friend, a gentleman, a "gentleman of the shade," and a soldier; he even enjoys turning the tables with "Thou hast done much harm upon me, Hal . . . I must give over this life, and I will give it over . . . I'll be damn'd for never a king's son in Christendom" (I.ii.102–9). It is the essence of his character, and his role, in *Part One,* that he never comes to rest where we can see him for what he "is." He is always in motion, always adopting postures, assuming characters.

That he does indeed care for Hal can be conveyed in performance without imposing sentimental tableaux on the action, provided that actors and producer recognize that he cares for the prince after his own fashion. It is from the prince that he chiefly gets his meaning, as it is from real kings that mock kings always get their meaning. We can believe it when we hear in *Henry V* that banishment has "killed his heart" (II.i.92). But to make much of a personal affection for the prince is a misconceived way to find meaning in Falstaff. His extraordinary meaningfulness comes from the way he manages to live "out of all order, out of all compass"

by his wit and his wits; and from the way he keeps reflecting on
the rest of the action, at first indirectly by the mock roles that he
plays, at the end directly by his comments at the battle. Through
this burlesque and mockery an intelligence of the highest order is
expressed. It is not always clear whether the intelligence is Falstaff's or the dramatist's; often the question need not arise. Romantic criticism went the limit in ascribing a God-like superiority
to the character, to the point of insisting that he tells the lies about
the multiplying men in buckram merely to amuse, that he knew
all the time at Gadshill that it was with Hal and Poins that he
fought. To go so far in that direction obviously destroys the
drama—spoils the joke in the case of the "incomprehensible lies,"
a joke which, as E. E. Stoll abundantly demonstrates, must be a
joke *on* Falstaff.[4] On the other hand, I see no reason why actor
and producer should not do all they can to make us enjoy the intellectual mastery involved in Falstaff's comic resource and power
of humorous redefinition. It is crucial that he should not be made
so superior that he is never in predicaments, for his genius is expressed in getting out of them. But he does have genius, as Maurice
Morgann rightly insisted though in a misconceived way. Through
his part Shakespeare expressed attitudes towards experience which,
grounded in a saturnalian reversal of values, went beyond that to
include a radical challenge to received ideas.

Throughout the first three acts of *Part One,* the Falstaff comedy
is continuously responsive to the serious action. There are constant
parallels and contrasts with what happens at court or with the
rebels. And yet these parallels are not explicitly noticed; the relations are presented, not formulated. So the first scene ends in a
mood of urgency, with the tired king urging haste: "come yourself with speed to us again." The second scene opens with Hal asking Falstaff "What a devil hast thou to do with the time of the day?"
The prose in which he explains why time is nothing to Sir John
is wonderfully leisurely and abundant, an elegant sort of talk that
has all the time in the world to enjoy the completion of its schema-
tized patterns:

> Unless hours were cups of sack, and minutes capons, and clocks the
> tongues of bawds, and dials the signs of leaping houses, and the blessed
> sun himself a fair hot wench in flame-colored taffeta, I see no reason
> why thou shouldst be so superfluous to demand the time of the day.
>
> (I.ii.7–13)

⁴ *Shakespeare Studies,* pp. 403–33.

The same difference in the attitude towards time runs throughout
and goes with the difference between verse and prose mediums. A
similar contrast obtains about lese majesty. Thus at their first appearance Falstaff insults Hal's majesty with casual, off-hand wit
which the prince tolerates (while getting his own back by jibing at
Falstaff's girth):

> And I prithee, sweet wag, when thou art king, as God save thy
> Grace—Majesty I should say, for grace thou wilt have none—
> *Prince.* What, none?
> *Falstaff.* No, by my troth; not so much as will serve to be prologue to
> an egg and butter.
> *Prince.* Well, how then? Come, roundly, roundly.   (I.ii.17–25)

In the next scene, we see Worcester calling into question the grace of
Bolingbroke, "that same greatness too which our own hands/Have
holp to make so portly" (I.iii.12–13). The King's response is immediate and drastic, and his lines point a moral that Hal seems to
be ignoring:

> Worcester, get thee gone; for I do see
> Danger and disobedience in thine eye.
> O, sir, your presence is too bold and peremptory,
> And majesty might never yet endure
> The moody frontier of a servant brow.   (I.iii.15–19)

Similar parallels run between Hotspur's heroics and Falstaff's mock-
heroics. In the third scene we hear Hotspur talking of "an easy
leap/To pluck bright honor from the pale-face'd moon" (I.iii.201–2).
Then in the robbery, Falstaff is complaining that "Eight yards
of uneven ground is threescore and ten miles afoot for me," and
asking "Have you any levers to lift me up again, being down?"
(II.ii.25–28, 36) After Hotspur enters exclaiming against the cowardly lord who has written that he will not join the rebellion,
we have Falstaff's entrance to the tune of "A plague of all cowards" (II.iv.127). And so on, and so on. Shakespeare's art has reached
the point where he makes everything foil to everything else. Hal's
imagery, in his soliloquy, shows the dramatist thinking about such
relations: "like bright metal on a sullen ground,/My reformation,
glitt'ring o'er my fault" (I.ii.236–37).

Now it is not true that Falstaff's impudence about Hal's grace
undercuts Bolingbroke's majesty, nor that Sir John's posturing as
a hero among cowards invalidates the heroic commitment Hotspur
expresses when he says "but I tell you, my lord fool, out of this

nettle, danger, we pluck this flower, safety" (II.iii.11–12). The
relationship is not one of a mocking echo. Instead, there is a certain
distance between the comic and serious strains which leaves room
for a complex interaction, organized by the crucial role of the prince.
We are invited, by the King's unfavorable comparison in the opening scene, to see the Prince in relation to Hotspur. And Hal himself, in the midst of his Boars Head revel, compares himself with
Hotspur. In telling Poins of his encounter with the drawers among
the hogsheads of the wine-cellar, he says "I have sounded the very
bass-string of humility," goes on to note what he has gained by it,
"I can drink with any tinker in his own language during my life,"
and concludes with "I tell thee, Ned, thou hast lost much honour
that thou wert not with me in this action" (II.iv.5, 20–24). His
mock-heroic way of talking about "this action" shows how well he
knows how to value it from a princely vantage. But the remark
cuts two ways. For running the gamut of society *is* an important
action: after their experiment with Francis and his "Anon, anon,
sir," the Prince exclaims:

> That ever this fellow should have fewer words than a parrot, and yet
> the son of a woman! . . . I am not yet of Percy's mind, the Hotspur of
> the North; he that kills me some six or seven dozen of Scots at a
> breakfast, washes his hands, and says to his wife, "Fie upon this quiet
> life! I want work." "O my sweet Harry," says she, "how many hast thou
> kill'd to-day?" "Give my roan horse a drench," says he, and answers
> "Some fourteen," an hour after, "a trifle, a trifle." I prithee call in
> Falstaff. I'll play Percy, and that damn'd brawn shall play Dame
> Mortimer his wife.   (II.iv.110–24)

It is the narrowness and obliviousness of the martial hero that Hal's
mockery brings out; here his awareness explicitly spans the distance
between the separate strains of the action; indeed, the distance is
made the measure of the kingliness of his nature. His "I am not
yet of Percy's mind" implies what he later promises his father (the
commercial image he employs reflects his ability to use, after his
father's fashion, the politician's calculation and indirection):

> Percy is but my factor, good my lord,
> To engross up glorious deeds on my behalf . . .
>
> (III.ii.147–48)

In the Boars Head Tavern scene, Hal never carries out the plan
of playing Percy to Falstaff's Dame Mortimer; in effect he has
played both their parts already in his snatch of mimicry. But Fal-

staff provides him with a continuous exercise in the consciousness that comes from playing at being what one is not, and from seeing through such playing.

Even here, where one world does comment on another explicitly, Hotspur's quality is not invalidated; rather, his achievement is *placed*. It is included within a wider field which contains also the drawers, mine host, Mistress Quickly, and by implication, not only "all the good lads of Eastcheap" but all the estates of England.[5] When we saw Hotspur and his Lady, he was not foolish, but delightful in his headlong, spontaneous way. His Lady has a certain pathos in the complaints which serve to convey how all absorbing his battle passion is. But the joke is with him as he mocks her:

> Love? I love thee not;
> I care not for thee, Kate. This is no world
> To play with mammets and to tilt with lips.
> We must have bloody noses and crack'd crowns,
> And pass them current, too. Gods me, my horse!
>
>   (II.iii.93–97)

One could make some very broad fun of Hotspur's preference for his horse over his wife. But there is nothing of the kind in Shakespeare: here and later, his treatment values the conversion of love into war as one of the important human powers. Hotspur has the fullness of life and the unforced integrity of the great aristocrat who has never known what it is to cramp his own style. His style shows it; he speaks the richest, freshest poetry of the play, in lines that take all the scope they need to fulfill feeling and perception:

> oft the teeming earth
> Is with a kind of colic pinch'd and vex'd
> By the imprisoning of unruly wind
> Within her womb, which, for enlargement striving,
> Shakes the old beldame earth and topples down
> Steeples and mossgrown towers. At your birth
> Our grandam earth, having this distemp'rature,
> In passion shook.
>   *Glendower.* Cousin, of many men
> I do not bear these crossings. Give me leave
> To tell you once again that at my birth
> The front of heaven was full of fiery shapes,

[5] See Empson, *Pastoral*, pp. 42 ff.

> The goats ran from the mountains, and the herds
> Were strangely clamorous to the frighted fields.
>
> (III.i.28–40)

The established life of moss-grown towers is in Percy's poetic speech, as the grazed-over Welsh mountains are in Glendower's. They are both strong; everybody in this play is strong in his own way. Hotspur's humor is untrammeled, like his verse, based on the heedless empiricism of an active, secure nobleman:

> *Glendower.* I can call spirits from the vasty deep.
> *Hotspur.* Why, so can I, or so can any man;
> But will they come when you do call for them?
>
> (III.i.53–55)

His unconsciousness makes him, at other moments, a comic if winning figure, as the limitations of his feudal virtues are brought out: his want of tact and judgment, his choleric man's forgetfulness, his sudden boyish habit of leaping to conclusions, the noble but also comical way he can be carried away by "imagination of some great exploit" (I.iii.199), or by indignation at "this vile politician, Bolingbroke" (I.iii.241). Professor Lily B. Campbell has demonstrated that the rebellion of the Northern Earls in 1570 was present for Shakespeare's audience in watching the Percy family in the play.[6] The remoteness of this rough north country life from the London world of his audience, as well as its aristocratic charm, are conveyed when Hotspur tells his wife that she swears "like a comfit-maker's wife,"

> As if thou ne'er walk'st further than Finsbury.
> Swear me, Kate, like a lady as thou art,
> A good mouth-filling oath; and leave "in sooth"
> And such protest of pepper gingerbread
> To velvet guards and Sunday citizens.   (III.i.255–59)

It is the various strengths of a stirring world, not deficiencies, which make the conflict in *1 Henry IV*. Even the humble carriers, and the professional thieves, are full of themselves and their business:

> I am joined with no foot land-rakers, no long-staff sixpenny strikers, none of these mad mustachio purple-hued maltworms; but with nobility and tranquillity, burgomasters and great oneyers, such as can hold in,

---

[6] Lily B. Campbell, *Shakespeare's Histories, Mirrors of Elizabethan Policy* (San Marino, 1947), pp. 229–38.

such as will strike sooner than speak, and speak sooner than drink, and
drink sooner than pray; and yet, zounds, I lie; for they pray continually
to their saint, the commonwealth, or rather, not pray to her, but prey
on her, for they ride up and down on her and make her their boots.

(II.i.81–91)

In his early history play, 2 *Henry VI,* as we have noticed, Shakespeare used his clowns to present the Jack Cade rebellion as a
saturnalia ignorantly undertaken in earnest, a highly-stylized piece
of dramaturgy, which he brings off triumphantly. In this more
complex play the underworld is presented as endemic disorder
alongside the crisis of noble rebellion: the king's lines are apposite
when he says that insurrection can always mobilize

> moody beggars, starving for a time
> Of pell-mell havoc and confusion.   (V.i.81–82)

Falstaff places himself in saying "Well, God be thanked for these
rebels. They offend none but the virtuous. I laud them, I praise
them."

The whole effect, in the opening acts, when there is little commentary on the spectacle as a whole, is of life overflowing its
bounds by sheer vitality. Thieves and rebels and honest men—"one
that hath abundance of charge too, God knows what" (II.i.64)—
ride up and down on the commonwealth, pray to her and prey on
her. Hotspur exults that "That roan shall be my throne" (II.iii.73).
Falstaff exclaims, "Shall I? Content. This chair shall be my state"
(II.iv.415). Hal summarizes the effect, after Hotspur is dead, with

> When that this body did contain a spirit,
> A kingdom for it was too small a bound.   (V.iv.89–90)

The stillness when he says this, at the close of the battle, is the
moment when his royalty is made manifest. When he stands poised
above the prostrate bodies of Hotspur and Falstaff, his position on
the stage and his lines about the two heroes express a nature which
includes within a larger order the now subordinated parts of life
which are represented in those two: in Hotspur, honor, the social
obligation to courage and self-sacrifice, a value which has been isolated in this magnificently anarchical feudal lord to become almost
everything; and in Falstaff, the complementary *joie de vivre* which
rejects all social obligations with "I like not such grinning honour
as Sir Walter hath. Give me life" (V.iii.61).

Getting Rid of Bad Luck by Comedy

But Falstaff does not stay dead. He jumps up in a triumph which, like Bottom coming alive after Pyramus is dead, reminds one of the comic resurrections in the St. George plays. He comes back to life because he is still relevant. His apology for counterfeiting cuts deeply indeed, because it does not apply merely to himself; we can relate it, as William Empson has shown, to the counterfeiting of the king. Bolingbroke too knows when it is time to counterfeit, both in this battle, where he survives because he has many marching in his coats, and throughout a political career where, as he acknowledges to Hal, he manipulates the symbols of majesty with a calculating concern for ulterior results. L. C. Knights, noticing this relation and the burlesque, elsewhere in Falstaff's part, of the attitudes of chivalry, concluded with nineteenth-century critics like Ulrici and Victor Hugo that the comedy should be taken as a devastating satire on war and government.[7] But this is obviously an impossible, anachronistic view, based on the assumption of the age of individualism that politics and war are unnatural activities that can be done without. Mr. Knights would have it that the audience should feel a jeering response when Henry sonorously declares, after Shrewsbury: "Thus ever did rebellion find rebuke." This interpretation makes a shambles of the heroic moments of the play—makes them clearly impossible to act. My own view, as will be clear, is that the dynamic relation of comedy and serious action is saturnalian rather than satiric, that the misrule works, through the whole dramatic rhythm, to consolidate rule. But it is also true, as Mr. Empson remarks, that "the double plot is carrying a fearful strain here."[8] Shakespeare is putting an enormous pressure on the comedy to resolve the challenge posed by the ironic perceptions presented in his historical action.

The process at work, here and earlier in the play, can be made clearer, I hope, by reference now to the carrying off of bad luck by the scapegoat of saturnalian ritual. We do not need to assume that Shakespeare had any such ritual patterns consciously in mind; whatever his conscious intention, it seems to me that these analogues illuminate patterns which his poetic drama presents concretely and dramatically. After such figures as the Mardi Gras or Carnival

---

[7] "A Note on Comedy," *Determinations,* ed. by F. R. Leavis (London, 1934).
[8] *Pastoral,* p. 46.

have presided over a revel, they are frequently turned on by their followers, tried in some sort of court, convicted of sins notorious in the village during the last year, and burned or buried in effigy to signify a new start. In other ceremonies described in *The Golden Bough,* mockery kings appear as recognizable substitutes for real kings, stand trial in their stead, and carry away the evils of their realms into exile or death. One such scapegoat figure, as remote historically as could be from Shakespeare, is the Tibetan King of the Years, who enjoyed ten days' misrule during the annual holiday of Buddhist monks at Lhasa. At the climax of his ceremony, after doing what he liked while collecting bad luck by shaking a black yak's tail over the people, he mounted the temple steps and ridiculed the representative of the Grand Llama, proclaiming heresies like "What we perceive through the five senses is no illusion. All you teach is untrue." A few minutes later, discredited by a cast of loaded dice, he was chased off to exile and possible death in the mountains.[9] One cannot help thinking of Falstaff's catechism on honor, spoken just before another valuation of honor is expressed in the elevated blank verse of a hero confronting death: "Can honour . . . take away the grief of a wound? No. . . . What is honour? a word. What is that word, honour? Air." Hal's final expulsion of Falstaff appears in the light of these analogies to carry out an impersonal pattern, not merely political but ritual in character. After the guilty reign of Bolingbroke, the prince is making a fresh start as the new king. At a level beneath the moral notions of a personal reform, we can see a nonlogical process of purification by sacrifice— the sacrifice of Falstaff. The career of the old king, a successful usurper whose conduct of affairs has been sceptical and opportunistic, has cast doubt on the validity of the whole conception of a divinely-ordained and chivalrous kingship to which Shakespeare and his society were committed. And before Bolingbroke, Richard II had given occasion for doubts about the rituals of kingship in an opposite way, by trying to use them magically. Shakespeare had shown Richard assuming that the symbols of majesty should be absolutes, that the names of legitimate power should be transcendently effective regardless of social forces. Now both these attitudes have been projected also in Falstaff; he carries to comically delightful and degraded extremes both a magical use of moral sanctions and the complementary opportunistic manipulation and scepticism. So the ritual analogy suggests that by turning on Falstaff as a scapegoat, as the villagers turned on their Mardi Gras, the prince can

[9] See James G. Frazer, *The Scapegoat* (London, 1914), pp. 218–23 and passim.

free himself from the sins, the "bad luck," of Richard's reign and of his father's reign, to become a king in whom chivalry and a sense of divine ordination are restored.

But this process of carrying off bad luck, if it is to be made *dramatically* cogent, as a symbolic action accomplished in and by dramatic form, cannot take place magically in Shakespeare's play. When it happens magically in the play, we have, I think, a failure to transform ritual into comedy. In dealing with fully successful comedy, the magical analogy is only a useful way of organizing our awareness of a complex symbolic action. The expulsion of evil works as dramatic form only in so far as it is realized in a movement from participation to rejection which happens, moment by moment, in our response to Falstaff's clowning misrule. We watch Falstaff adopt one posture after another, in the effort to give himself meaning at no cost; and moment by moment we see that the meaning is specious. So our participation is repeatedly diverted to laughter. The laughter, disbursing energy originally mobilized to respond to a valid meaning, signalizes our mastery by understanding of the tendency which has been misapplied or carried to an extreme.

Consider, for example, the use of magical notions of royal power in the most famous of all Falstaff's burlesques:

> By the Lord, I knew ye as well as he that made ye. . . . Was it for me to kill the heir apparent? Should I turn upon the true prince? Why, thou knowest I am as valiant as Hercules; but beware instinct. The lion will not touch the true prince. Instinct is a great matter. I was now a coward on instinct. I shall think the better of myself, and thee, during my life—I for a valiant lion, and thou for a true prince. But, by the Lord, lads, I am glad you have the money. Hostess, clap to the doors: watch to-night, pray to-morrow.   (II.iv.295–306)

Here Falstaff has recourse to the brave conception that legitimate kingship has a magical potency. This is the sort of absolutist appeal to sanctions which Richard II keeps falling back on in his desperate "conjuration" (*R.II* III.ii.23) by hyperbole:

> So when this thief, this traitor, Bolingbroke, . . .
> Shall see us rising in our throne, the East,
> His treasons will sit blushing in his face,
> Not able to endure the sight of day. . . .
> The breath of worldly men cannot depose
> The deputy elected by the Lord.
> For every man that Bolingbroke hath press'd
> To lift shrewd steel against our golden crown,

> God for his Richard hath in heavenly pay
> A glorious angel.   (*R.II* III.ii.47–61)

In Richard's case, a tragic irony enforces the fact that heavenly angels are of no avail if one's coffers are empty of golden angels and the Welsh army have dispersed. In Falstaff's case, the irony is comically obvious, the "lies are like the father that begets them; gross as a mountain, open, palpable" (II.iv.249–50). Hal stands for the judgment side of our response, while Falstaff embodies the enthusiastic, irrepressible conviction of fantasy's omnipotence. The Prince keeps returning to Falstaff's bogus "instinct"; "Now, sirs . . . You are lions too, you ran away upon instinct, you will not touch the true prince; no—fie!" (II.iv.29–34) After enjoying the experience of seeing through such notions of magical majesty, he is never apt to make the mistake of assuming that, just because he is king, lions like Northumberland will not touch him. King Richard's bad luck came precisely from such an assumption—unexamined, of course, as fatal assumptions always are. Freud's account of bad luck, in *The Psychopathology of Everyday Life*, sees it as the expression of unconscious motives which resist the conscious goals of the personality. This view helps to explain how the acting out of disruptive motives in saturnalia or in comedy can serve to master potential aberration by revaluing it in relation to the whole of experience. So Falstaff, in acting out this absolutist aberration, is taking away what might have been Hal's bad luck, taking it away not in a magical way, but by extending the sphere of conscious control. The comedy is a civilized equivalent of the primitive rite. A similar mastery of potential aberration is promoted by the experience of seeing through Falstaff's burlesque of the sort of headlong chivalry presented seriously in Hotspur.

In order to put the symbolic action of the comedy in larger perspective, it will be worth while to consider further, for a moment, the relation of language to stage action and dramatic situation in *Richard II*. That play is a pioneering exploration of the semantics of royalty, shot through with talk about the potency and impotence of language. In the first part, we see a Richard who is possessor of an apparently magical omnipotence: for example, when he commutes Bolingbroke's banishment from ten to six years, Bolingbroke exclaims:

> How long a time lies in one little word;
> Four lagging winters and four wanton springs
> End in a word: such is the breath of kings.
>
> (*R.II* I.iii.213–15)

Richard assumes he has such magic breath inevitably, regardless of "the breath of worldly men." When he shouts things like "Is not the king's name twenty thousand names?/Arm, arm, my name!" he carries the absolutist assumption to the giddiest verge of absurdity. When we analyze the magical substitution of words for things in such lines, looking at them from outside the rhythm of feeling in which they occur, it seems scarcely plausible that a drama should be built around the impulse to adopt such an assumption. It seems especially implausible in our own age, when we are so conscious, on an abstract level, of the dependence of verbal efficacy on the social group. The analytical situation involves a misleading perspective, however; for, whatever your assumptions about semantics, when you have to *act*, to *be* somebody or become somebody, there is a moment when you have to have faith that the unknown world beyond will respond to the names you commit yourself to as right names.[10] The Elizabethan mind, moreover, generally assumed that one played one's part in a divinely ordained pageant where each man *was* his name and the role his name implied. The expression of this faith, and of the outrage of it is particularly drastic in the Elizabethan drama, which can be regarded, from this vantage, as an art form developed to express the shock and exhilaration of the discovery that life is not pageantry. As Professor Tillyard has pointed out, *Richard II* is the most ceremonial of all Shakespeare's plays, and the ceremony all comes to nothing.[11] In Richard's deposition scene, one way in which anguish at his fall is expressed is by a focus on his loss of names: he responds to Northumberland's "My Lord—" by flinging out

> No lord of thine, thou haught insulting man,
> Nor no man's lord. I have no name, no title—
> No, not that name was given me at the font—
> But 'tis usurp'd. Alack the heavy day,
> That I have worn so many winters out
> And know not now what name to call myself!
> O that I were a mockery king of snow,
> Standing before the sun of Bolingbroke
> To melt myself away in water-drops! (*R.II* IV.i.253–62)

His next move is to call for the looking glass in which he stares

---

[10] I am indebted to my colleagues Professor Theodore Baird and Professor G. Armour Craig for this way of seeing the relation of names to developing situations.

[11] See *Shakespeare's History Plays* (New York, 1946), pp. 245 ff.

at his face to look for the meaning the face has lost. To lose one's
meaning, one's social role, is to be reduced to mere body.

Here again the tragedy can be used to illuminate the comedy.
Since the Elizabethan drama was a double medium of words and
of physical gestures, it frequently expressed the pathos of the loss
of meaning by emphasizing moments when word and gesture, name
and body, no longer go together, just as it presented the excitement
of a gain of meaning by showing a body seizing on names when
a hero creates his identity. In the deposition scene, Richard says
"mark me how I will undo myself" (IV.i.203). Then he gives away
by physical gestures the symbolic meanings which have constituted
that self. When at last he has no name, the anguish is that the
face, the body, remain when the meaning is gone. There is also
something in Richard's lines which, beneath the surface of his self-
pity, relishes such undoing, a self-love which looks towards fulfill-
ment in that final reduction of all to the body which is death. This
narcissistic need for the physical is the other side of the attitude that
the magic of the crown should altogether transcend the physical—
and the human:

> Cover your heads, and mock not flesh and blood
> With solemn reverence. Throw away respect,
> Tradition, form, and ceremonious duty;
> For you have but mistook me all this while.
> I live with bread like you, feel want, taste grief,
> Need friends. Subjected thus,
> How can you say to me I am a king?   (*R.II* III.ii.171–77)

In expressing the disappointment of Richard's magical expectations,
as well as their sweeping magnificence, the lines make manifest
the aberration which is mastered in the play by tragic form.

The same sort of impulse is expressed and mastered by comic
form in the Henry IV comedy. When Richard wishes he were a
mockery king of snow, to melt before the sun of Bolingbroke, the
image expresses on one side the wish to escape from the body
with which he is left when his meaning has gone—to weep himself
away in water drops. But the lines also look wistfully towards
games of mock royalty where, since the whole thing is based on
snow, the collapse of meaning need not hurt. Falstaff is such a
mockery king. To be sure, he is flesh and blood, of a kind: he is
tallow, anyway. He "sweats to death/And lards the lean earth as
he walks along." Of course he is not just a mockery, not just his
role, not just bombast. Shakespeare, as always, makes the symbolic
role the product of a life which includes contradictions of it, such

as the morning-after regrets when Falstaff thinks of the inside of
a church and notices that his skin hangs about him like an old
lady's loose gown. Falstaff is human enough so that "Were't not
for laughing, . . . [we] should pity him." But we do laugh, because
when Falstaff's meanings collapse, little but make-believe has been
lost:

> *Prince.* Thy state is taken for a join'd-stool, thy golden sceptre for a
> leaden dagger, and thy precious rich crown for a pitiful bald crown.
>
> (II.iv.418–20)

Falstaff's effort to make his body and furnishings mean sovereignty
is doomed from the start; he must work with a leaden dagger, the
equivalent of a Vice's dagger of lath. But Falstaff does have golden
words, and an inexhaustible vitality in using them. He can name
himself nobly, reordering the world by words so as to do himself
credit:

> No, my good lord. Banish Peto, banish Bardolph, banish Poins; but for
> sweet Jack Falstaff, kind Jack Falstaff, true Jack Falstaff, valiant Jack
> Falstaff, and therefore more valiant being, as he is, old Jack Falstaff,
> banish not him thy Harry's company, banish not him thy Harry's
> company. Banish plump Jack, and banish all the world!
>
> (II.iv.519–27)

I quote such familiar lines to recall their effect of incantation:
they embody an effort at a kind of magical naming. Each repetition
of "sweet Jack Falstaff, kind Jack Falstaff" aggrandizes an identity
which the serial clauses caress and cherish. At the very end, in
"plump Jack," the disreputable belly is glorified.

In valid heroic and majestic action, the bodies of the personages
are constantly being elevated by becoming the vehicles of social
meanings; in the comedy, such elevation becomes burlesque, and
in the repeated failures to achieve a fusion of body and symbol,
abstract meanings keep falling back into the physical. "A plague
of sighing and grief! it blows a man up like a bladder" (II.iv.365–
66). The repetition of such joking about Falstaff's belly makes it
meaningful in a very special way, as a symbol of the process of
inflation and collapse of meaning. So it represents the power of the
individual life to continue despite the collapse of social roles. This
continuing on beyond definitions is after all what we call "the
body" in one main meaning of the term: Falstaff's belly is thus the
essence of body—an essence which can be defined only dynamically,
by failures of meaning. The effect of indestructible vitality is reinforced by the association of Falstaff's figure with the gay eating

and drinking of Shrove Tuesday and Carnival. Whereas, in the tragedy, the reduction is to a body which can only die, here reduction is to a body which typifies our power to eat and drink our way through a shambles of intellectual and moral contradictions.

So we cannot resist sharing Falstaff's genial self-love when he commends his vision of plump Jack to the Prince, just as we share the ingenuous self-love of a little child. But the dramatist is ever on the alert to enforce the ironies that dog the tendency of fantasy to equate the self with "all the world." So a most monstrous watch comes beating at the doors which have been clapped to against care; everyday breaks in on holiday.

The Rejection of Falstaff

by A. C. Bradley

Up to a certain point Falstaff is ludicrous in the same way as
many other figures, his distinction lying, so far, chiefly in the mere
abundance of ludicrous traits. Why we should laugh at a man with
a huge belly and corresponding appetites; at the inconveniences he
suffers on a hot day, or in playing the footpad, or when he falls
down and there are no levers at hand to lift him up again; at the
incongruity of his unwieldy bulk and the nimbleness of his spirit,
the infirmities of his age and his youthful lightness of heart; at the
enormity of his lies and wiles, and the suddenness of their exposure
and frustration; at the contrast between his reputation and his real
character, seen most absurdly when, at the mere mention of his
name, a redoubted rebel surrenders to him—why, I say, we should
laugh at these and many such things, this is no place to inquire;
but unquestionably we do. Here we have them poured out in end-
less profusion and with that air of careless ease which is so fascinating in Shakespeare; and with the enjoyment of them I believe
many readers stop. But while they are quite essential to the character, there is in it much more. For these things by themselves do
not explain why, besides laughing at Falstaff, we are made happy
by him and laugh *with* him. He is not, like Parolles, a mere *object*
of mirth.

The main reason why he makes us so happy and puts us so entirely at our ease is that he himself is happy and entirely at his
ease. "Happy" is too weak a word; he is in bliss, and we share his
glory. Enjoyment—no fitful pleasure crossing a dull life, nor any
vacant convulsive mirth—but a rich deep-toned chuckling enjoyment circulates continually through all his being. If you ask *what*
he enjoys, no doubt the answer is, in the first place, eating and
drinking, taking his ease at his inn, and the company of other

From "The Rejection of Falstaff," by A. C. Bradley. From Oxford Lectures
on Poetry (London: Macmillan & Co., Ltd., 1959), pp. 260–64, 269–73. Reprinted
by permission of St. Martin's Press, Inc. and Macmillan & Co., Ltd.

merry souls. Compared with these things, what we count the graver
interests of life are nothing to him. But then, while we are under
his spell, it is impossible to consider these graver interests; gravity
is to us, as to him, inferior to gravy; and what he does enjoy he
enjoys with such a luscious and good-humoured zest that we sympa-
thise and he makes us happy. And if any one objected, we should
answer with Sir Toby Belch, "Dost thou think, because thou art
virtuous, there shall be no more cakes and ale?"

But this, again, is far from all. Falstaff's ease and enjoyment are
not simply those of the happy man of appetite; they are those of the
humorist, and the humorist of genius. Instead of being comic to
you and serious to himself, he is more ludicrous to himself than to
you; and he makes himself out more ludicrous than he is, in order
that he and others may laugh. Prince Hal never made such sport of
Falstaff's person as he himself did. It is *he* who says that his skin
hangs about him like an old lady's loose gown, and that he walks
before his page like a sow that hath o'erwhelmed all her litter but
one. And he jests at himself when he is alone just as much as when
others are by. It is the same with his appetites. The direct enjoyment they bring him is scarcely so great as the enjoyment of
laughing at this enjoyment; and for all his addiction to sack you
never see him for an instant with a brain dulled by it, or a temper
turned solemn, silly, quarrelsome, or pious. The virtue it instils
into him, of filling his brain with nimble, fiery, and delectable
shapes—this, and his humorous attitude towards it, free him, in a
manner, from slavery to it; and it is this freedom, and no secret
longing for better things (those who attribute such a longing to him
are far astray), that makes his enjoyment contagious and prevents
our sympathy with it from being disturbed.

The bliss of freedom gained in humour is the essence of Falstaff.
His humour is not directed only or chiefly against obvious absurdities; he is the enemy of everything that would interfere with his
ease, and therefore of anything serious, and especially of everything
respectable and moral. For these things impose limits and obligations, and make us the subjects of old father antic the law, and
the categorical imperative, and our station and its duties, and conscience, and reputation, and other people's opinions, and all sorts
of nuisances. I say he is therefore their enemy; but I do him wrong;
to say that he is their enemy implies that he regards them as serious
and recognises their power, when in truth he refuses to recognise
them at all. They are to him absurd; and to reduce a thing *ad
absurdum* is to reduce it to nothing and to walk about free and
rejoicing. This is what Falstaff does with all the would-be serious

things of life, sometimes only by his words, sometimes by his actions
too. He will make truth appear absurd by solemn statements, which
he utters with perfect gravity and which he expects nobody to believe; and honour, by demonstrating that it cannot set a leg, and
that neither the living nor the dead can possess it; and law, by
evading all the attacks of its highest representative and almost
forcing him to laugh at his own defeat; and patriotism, by filling
his pockets with the bribes offered by competent soldiers who want
to escape service, while he takes in their stead the halt and maimed
and the gaol-birds; and duty, by showing how he labours in his
vocation—of thieving; and courage, alike by mocking at his own
capture of Colvile and gravely claiming to have killed Hotspur;
and war, by offering the Prince his bottle of sack when he is asked
for a sword; and religion, by amusing himself with remorse at odd
times when he has nothing else to do; and the fear of death, by
maintaining perfectly untouched, in the face of imminent peril and
even while he *feels* the fear of death, the very same power of dissolving it in persiflage that he shows when he sits at ease in his
inn. These are the wonderful achievements which he performs, not
with the discontent of a cynic, but with the gaiety of a boy. And,
therefore, we praise him, we laud him, for he offends none but the
virtuous, and denies that life is real or life is earnest, and delivers
us from the oppression of such nightmares, and lifts us into the
atmosphere of perfect freedom.

No one in the play understands Falstaff fully, any more than
Hamlet was understood by the persons round him. They are both
men of genius. Mrs. Quickly and Bardolph are his slaves, but they
know not why. "Well, fare thee well," says the hostess whom he has
pillaged and forgiven; "I have known thee these twenty-nine years,
come peas-cod time, but an honester and truer-hearted man—well,
fare thee well." Poins and the Prince delight in him; they get him
into corners for the pleasure of seeing him escape in ways they cannot imagine; but they often take him much too seriously. Poins,
for instance, rarely sees, the Prince does not always see, and mor-
alising critics never see, that when Falstaff speaks ill of a companion
behind his back, or writes to the Prince that Poins spreads it abroad
that the Prince is to marry his sister, he knows quite well that what
he says will be repeated, or rather, perhaps, is absolutely indifferent
whether it be repeated or not, being certain that it can only give
him an opportunity for humour. It is the same with his lying, and
almost the same with his cowardice, the two main vices laid to his
charge even by sympathisers. Falstaff is neither a liar nor a coward
in the usual sense, like the typical cowardly boaster of comedy. He

tells his lies either for their own humour, or on purpose to get himself into a difficulty. He rarely expects to be believed, perhaps never. He abandons a statement or contradicts it the moment it is made. There is scarcely more intent in his lying than in the humorous exaggerations which he pours out in soliloquy just as much as when others are by. Poins and the Prince understand this in part. You see them waiting eagerly to convict him, not that they may really put him to shame, but in order to enjoy the greater lie that will swallow up the less. But their sense of humour lags behind his. Even the Prince seems to accept as half-serious that remorse of his which passes so suddenly into glee at the idea of taking a purse, and his request to his friend to bestride him if he should see him down in the battle. Bestride Falstaff! "Hence! Wilt thou lift up Olympus" . . . ?

The main source, then, of our sympathetic delight in Falstaff is his humorous superiority to everything serious, and the freedom of soul enjoyed in it. But, of course, this is not the whole of his character. Shakespeare knew well enough that perfect freedom is not to be gained in this manner; we are ourselves aware of it even while we are sympathising with Falstaff; and as soon as we regard him seriously it becomes obvious. His freedom is limited in two main ways. For one thing he cannot rid himself entirely of respect for all that he professes to ridicule. He shows a certain pride in his rank: unlike the Prince, he is haughty to the drawers, who call him a proud Jack. He is not really quite indifferent to reputation. When the Chief Justice bids him pay his debt to Mrs. Quickly for his reputation's sake, I think he feels a twinge, though to be sure he proceeds to pay her by borrowing from her. He is also stung by any thoroughly serious imputation on his courage, and winces at the recollection of his running away on Gadshill; he knows that his behaviour there certainly looked cowardly, and perhaps he remembers that he would not have behaved so once. It is, further, very significant that, for all his dissolute talk, he has never yet allowed the Prince and Poins to *see* him as they saw him afterwards with Doll Tearsheet; not, of course, that he has any moral shame in the matter, but he knows that in such a situation he, in his old age, must appear contemptible—not a humorist but a mere object of mirth. And, finally, he has affection in him—affection, I think, for Poins and Bardolph, and certainly for the Prince; and that is a thing which he cannot jest out of existence. Hence, as the effect of his rejection shows, he is not really invulnerable. And then, in the second place, since he is in the flesh, his godlike freedom has consequences and conditions; consequences, for there is something painfully wrong with his great toe; conditions, for he cannot eat and drink forever without money, and his purse suffers from consumption, a disease for which he can find no remedy. As the Chief Justice tells him, his means are very slender and his waste great; and his answer, "I would it were otherwise; I would my means were greater and my waist slenderer," though worth much money, brings none in. And so he is driven to evil deeds; not only to cheating his tailor like a gentleman, but to fleecing Justice Shallow, and to highway robbery, and to cruel depredations on the poor woman whose affection he has secured. All this is perfectly consistent with the other side of his character, but by itself it makes an ugly picture.

Yes, it makes an ugly picture when you look at it seriously. But then, surely, so long as the humorous atmosphere is preserved and the humorous attitude maintained, you do not look at it so. You no more regard Falstaff's misdeeds morally than you do the much more atrocious misdeeds of Punch or Reynard the Fox. You do not exactly ignore them, but you attend only to their comic aspect. This is the very spirit of comedy, and certainly of Shakespeare's comic world, which is one of make-believe, not merely as his tragic world is, but in a further sense—a world in which gross improbabilities are accepted with a smile, and many things are welcomed as merely laughable which, regarded gravely, would excite anger and disgust. The intervention of a serious spirit breaks up such a world, and would destroy our pleasure in Falstaff's company. Accordingly through the greater part of these dramas Shakespeare carefully confines this spirit to the scenes of war and policy, and dismisses it entirely in the humorous parts. Hence, if *Henry IV* had been a comedy like *Twelfth Night,* I am sure that he would no more have ended it with the painful disgrace of Falstaff than he ended *Twelfth Night* by disgracing Sir Toby Belch.

But *Henry IV* was to be in the main a historical play, and its chief hero Prince Henry. In the course of it his greater and finer qualities were to be gradually revealed, and it was to end with beautiful scenes of reconciliation and affection between his father and him, and a final emergence of the wild Prince as a just, wise, stern, and glorious King. Hence, no doubt, it seemed to Shakespeare that Falstaff at last must be disgraced, and must therefore appear no longer as the invincible humorist, but as an object of ridicule and even of aversion. And probably also his poet's insight showed him that Henry, as he conceived him, *would* behave harshly to Falstaff in order to impress the world, especially when his mind had been wrought to a high pitch by the scene with his dying father and the impression of his own solemn consecration to great duties.

This conception was a natural and a fine one; and if the execution was not an entire success, it is yet full of interest. Shakespeare's purpose being to work a gradual change in our feelings towards Falstaff, and to tinge the humorous atmosphere more and more deeply with seriousness, we see him carrying out this purpose in the Second Part of *Henry IV*. Here he separates the Prince from Falstaff as much as he can, thus withdrawing him from Falstaff's influence, and weakening in our minds the connection between the two. In the First Part we constantly see them together; in the Second (it is a remarkable fact) only once before the rejection. Further, in the scenes where Henry appears apart from Falstaff, we watch him growing more and more grave, and awakening more and more poetic interest; while Falstaff, though his humour scarcely flags to the end, exhibits more and more of his seamy side. This is nowhere turned to the full light in Part One; but in Part Two we see him as the heartless destroyer of Mrs. Quickly, as a ruffian seriously defying the Chief Justice because his position as an officer on service gives him power to do wrong, as the pike preparing to snap up the poor old dace Shallow, and (this is the one scene where Henry and he meet) as the worn-out lecher, not laughing at his servitude to the flesh but sunk in it. Finally, immediately before the rejection, the world where he is king is exposed in all its sordid criminality when we find Mrs. Quickly and Doll arrested for being concerned in the death of one man, if not more, beaten to death by their bullies; and the dangerousness of Falstaff is emphasised in his last words as he hurries from Shallow's house to London, words at first touched with humour but at bottom only too seriously meant: "Let us take any man's horses; the laws of England are at my commandment. Happy are they which have been my friends, and woe unto my Lord Chief Justice." His dismissal to the Fleet by the Chief Justice is the dramatic vengeance for that threat.

Yet all these excellent devices fail. They cause us momentary embarrassment at times when repellent traits in Falstaff's character are disclosed; but they fail to change our attitude of humour into one of seriousness, and our sympathy into repulsion. And they were bound to fail, because Shakespeare shrank from adding to them the one device which would have ensured success. If, as the Second Part of *Henry IV* advanced, he had clouded over Falstaff's humour so heavily that the man of genius turned into the Falstaff of the *Merry Wives*, we should have witnessed his rejection without a pang. This Shakespeare was too much of an artist to do—though even in this way he did something—and without this device he could not succeed. As I said, in the creation of Falstaff he overreached himself. He was caught up on the wind of his own genius, and carried so far that he could not descend to earth at the intended spot. It is not a misfortune that happens to many authors, nor is it one we can regret, for it costs us but a trifling inconvenience in one scene, while we owe to it perhaps the greatest comic character in literature. For it is in this character, and not in the judgment he brings upon Falstaff's head, that Shakespeare asserts his supremacy. To show that Falstaff's freedom of soul was in part illusory, and that the realities of life refused to be conjured away by his humour—this was what we might expect from Shakespeare's unfailing sanity, but it was surely no achievement beyond the power of lesser men. The achievement was Falstaff himself, and the conception of that freedom of soul, a freedom illusory only in part, and attainable only by a mind which had received from Shakespeare's own the inexplicable touch of infinity which he bestowed on Hamlet and Macbeth and Cleopatra, but denied to Henry the Fifth.

The Ambiguity of Falstaff

by William Empson

. . . This story of a prodigal who became a hero was already very rich when Shakespeare took it over or "cashed in on it"; it was the most popular part of the History series and carried a variety of implications, all the more because it was taken easily as a joke. To replan the trilogy on the basis of leaving some of them out, and that is really what Mr. Dover Wilson is up to, is sure to mislead; also I find it odd of him to claim that a historical point of view is what makes him treat Falstaff as medieval rather than Renaissance. Of course this does not make me deny that the medieval elements are still there. Falstaff is in part simply a "Vice," that is, an energetic symbol of impulses which most people have to repress, who gives pleasure by at once releasing and externalizing them. His plausibility is amusing, and his incidental satire on the world can be accepted as true, but what he stands for is recognized as wrong, and he must be punished in the end. Also (as a minor version of this type) he is in part the "cowardly swashbuckler," of the Latin play rather than the Miracle Play, whose absurdity and eventual exposure are to comfort the audience for their frequent anxiety and humiliation from "swashbucklers." As part of the historical series, he stands for the social disorder which is sure to be produced by a line of usurpers, therefore he is a parallel to the rebel leaders though very unlike them; the good king must shake him off in the end as part of his work of reuniting the country. Also I think there is a more timeless element about him, neither tied to his period in the story nor easily called Renaissance or medieval, though it seems to start with Shakespeare; he is the scandalous upper-class man whose behavior embarrasses his class and thereby pleases the lower class in the audience, as an "exposure"; the faint echoes of upper-class complaints about him, as in the change of his name, are I think

"The Ambiguity of Falstaff" [*editor's title*]. *From "Falstaff and Mr. Dover Wilson," by William Empson. From* Kenyon Review, *XV (Spring, 1953), 244–46, 255–57, 261–62. Reprinted by permission of the* Kenyon Review.

evidence that this was felt. For these last two functions, cowardice is not the vice chiefly required of him. But surely we have no reason to doubt that there were other forces at work behind the popularity of the myth, which can more directly be called Renaissance; something to do with greater trust in the natural man or pleasure in contemplating him, which would join on to what so many critics have said about "the comic idealization of freedom." I think it needs putting in more specific terms, but I don't see that Mr. Dover Wilson can be plausible in denying it altogether.

The most important "Renaissance" aspects of Falstaff, I think, can be most quickly described as nationalism and Machiavellianism; both of them make him a positively good tutor for a prince, as he regularly claims to be, so that it is not surprising that he produced a good King or that his rejection, though necessary, could be presented as somehow tragic. The Machiavellian view (no more tied to that author then than it is now, but more novel and shocking than it is now) is mainly the familiar one that a young man is better for "sowing his wild oats," especially if he is being trained to "handle men." The sort of ruler you can trust, you being one of the ruled, the sort that can understand his people, can lead them to glory, is one who has learned the world by experience, especially rather low experience; he knows the tricks, he can allow for human failings, and somehow between the two he can gauge the spirit of a situation or a period. The idea is not simply that Falstaff is debauched and tricky, though that in itself made him give Hal experience, and hardly any price was too high to pay for getting a good ruler, but that he had the breadth of mind and of social understanding which the Magnanimous Man needed to acquire. It seems a lower-class rather than upper-class line of thought (it is, of course, militantly anti-puritan, as we can assume the groundlings tended to be), and Falstaff can be regarded as a parody of it rather than a coarse acceptance of it by Shakespeare; but surely it is obviously present; indeed I imagine that previous critics have thought it too obvious to be worth writing down—there was no need to, till Mr. Dover Wilson began preaching at us about his Medieval Vice and his Ideal King. . . .

Returning to Falstaff's heart, I think there is a quick answer to the idea that the old brute had no heart, and therefore could not have died of breaking it. If he had had no heart he would have had no power, not even to get a drink, and he had a dangerous amount of power. I am not anxious to present Falstaff's heart as a very attractive object; you might say that it had better be called his vanity, but we are none of us sure how we would emerge from a

thorough analysis on those lines; the point is that everybody felt it
obvious that he had got one—otherwise he would not be plausible
even in attracting his young thieves, let alone his insanely devoted
"hostess." I daresay that the wincing away from the obvious (or from
Mr. Wyndham Lewis' account) which I seem to find in recent critics
is due to distaste for homosexuality, which is regarded nowadays in
more practical terms than the Victorian ones; the idea of Falstaff
making love to the Prince, they may feel, really has to be resisted.
But surely Johnson gives us the right perspective here; Falstaff felt
in himself the pain of a deformity which the audience could always
see; no amount of expression of love from Falstaff to his young
thieves would excite suspicion on that topic from the audience, not
because the audiences were innocent about it, but because they could
assume that any coming thief (let alone the Prince) would be too vain
to yield to such deformity. I agree that a doubt here could not have
been allowed, but there was no need to guard against it. A resistance
to it should not prevent us from noticing that Falstaff is rather
noisily shocked if young men do not love him. It is as well to take
an example from near the end of Part Two, where on Mr. Dover
Wilson's account there should be practically nothing left in him but
degeneration. He complains about Prince John (IV.ii.82), "this same
sober-blooded young boy doth not love me, nor a man cannot make
him laugh," and goes on in a fairly long speech to claim that he has
taught Prince Hal better humanity. This is easily thought ridiculous
because it is almost entirely a praise of drink, but the mere length
presumes dramatic effect; and drink was presumed to teach both
sympathy and courage (it is the combination of these two ideas in a
"heart," of course, which make it rather baffling to discuss what kind
of heart Falstaff has); and we have just seen Prince John perform
a disgusting act of cowardly treachery. This detail of structure, I
think, is enough to prove that at least the popular side of the
audience was assumed to agree with Falstaff. Indeed, if you compare
Hal to his brother and his father, whom the plays describe so very
unflinchingly, it is surely obvious that to love Falstaff was a liberal
education for him.

It is hard to defend this strange figure without doing it too much.
May I remind the patient reader that I am still doing what this essay
started to do, trying to show that Falstaff from his first conception
was not intended to arrive at Agincourt, because the Prince was
intended to reach that triumph over his broken heart. The real case
for rejecting Falstaff at the end of Part Two is that he was dangerously strong, indeed almost a rebel leader; Mr. Dover Wilson makes
many good points here, and he need not throw the drama away by

pretending that the bogey was always ridiculous. He is quite right in insisting that the Prince did not appear malicious in the rejection, and did only what was necessary; because Falstaff's expectations were enormous (and were recklessly expressed, by the way, to persons who could shame him afterwards); the terrible sentence "the laws of England are at my commandment, and woe to my Lord Chief Justice" meant something so practical to the audience that they may actually have stopped cracking nuts to hear what happened next. A mob would enter the small capital to see the coronation, and how much of it Falstaff could raise would be a reasonable subject for doubt; he could become "protector" of the young king; once you admit that he is both an aristocrat and a mob leader he is a familiar very dangerous type. . . .

I want finally to consider what the plays meant to Shakespeare himself, as apart from the audience; there is no very definite conclusion to be expected, but one ought not to talk as if an achievement on this scale has no personal backing. It seems that Shakespeare, though of course he won his position in the Company much earlier, already perhaps from the *Hen. VI* sequence, odd as it appears now, made his decisive position out of Falstaff. Not merely as a matter of money, which was very important, but also as a matter of trust from the audience, the triumph of Falstaff made possible the series of major tragedies; it was not merely an incident to him. I pursued the subject of the personal background to Falstaff in my *Pastoral* (pp. 102–9), and want to remark that I still agree with what I said there, though this essay is concerned with something rather different. Indeed I think that to understand the many-sidedness of the legend he was using makes it more plausible to think he felt his own experience to be an illustration of it. I proved, I think, that the first soliloquy of the Prince, assuring the audience that he was going to abandon his low friends, is drawn almost line by line from the Sonnets trying to justify the person addressed. It seems inherently probable that the humiliation of Shakespeare's dealings with his young patron, which one can guess were recently finished, would get thrown into the crucible in which the prince's friends had to be created. Falstaff looks to me like a secret comeback against aristocratic patrons, marking a recovery of nerve after a long attempt to be their hanger-on. But this was not done coarsely or with bad temper; the whole triumph of the thing, on its intimate side, was to turn his private humiliation into something very different and universally entertaining. I have been arguing that Falstaff is not meant to be socially low, even when he first appears, only to be a scandal to his rank; whereas Shakespeare of course had only a dubious profession and a suspect new gentility. There are warnings in the Sonnets that friendship with Shakespeare is bad for the patron's reputation, though we hardly ever get an actual admission of inferior social status (we do in the "dyer's hand"); he would rather talk obscurely about his "guilt." Snobbery, I think, had always seemed more real to him than self-righteousness, and even in the Sonnets we can see the beginning of the process that turned player Shakespeare into Falstaff, not a socially inferior friend but (what is much less painful) a scandalous one. Nobody would argue that the result is a life-like portrait of Shakespeare; though he must have known how to amuse, and talks in the Sonnets with a regret about his old age which was absurd even for Elizabethans if he was then under thirty-five, and undoubtedly was what they called a "villainist" tutor, the type who could give broad experience to a young prince. The point is not that he was like Falstaff but that, once he could imagine he was, once he could "identify" himself with a scandalous aristocrat, the sufferings of that character could be endured with positive glee. I am sure that is how he came to be liberated into putting such tremendous force into every corner of the picture.

The Turning Away of Prince Hal

by Jonas A. Barish

The rejection of Falstaff,[1] like much else in Shakespeare, has tended to turn a searchlight on us, and make ourselves reveal ourselves either as moralists or as sentimentalists. Shakespeare preserves such a delicate balance, throughout the two parts of *Henry IV*, between authority and rebellion, business and pleasure, sobriety and negligence, that the final episode almost invites us to view them in the light of our own deep preferences. If we range ourselves naturally on the side of authority, with its promise of order and justice, we will tend to endorse the casting off of the embodiment of disorder, the enemy-in-chief of the Lord Chief Justice. We will be gratified by the reckoning with misrule that has been so long in coming. We will subscribe to the authorized versions of the incident —to Prince John of Lancaster's opinion, for example, that his brother, the new king, has behaved handsomely to his old associates. If, on the other hand, our instincts prompt us to range ourselves more strongly on the side of freedom and spontaneity, we may tend to remember the vitality in Falstaff more than his lawlessness; we may recall his panegyric to sack more vividly than his fleecing of Shallow, and we will doubtless compare it in its favor with the official treachery practised by Prince John in Gaultree Forest. We will then find the rejection scene an affront, Hal a preaching humbug, and the whole episode a distasteful illustration of the incompatibility of kingship with kindness.[2]

From "The Turning Away of Prince Hal," by Jonas A. Barish. From Shakespeare Studies, I (1965), ed J. Leeds Barroll, 3rd (Cincinnati, Ohio: The University of Cincinnati,, 1965), pp. 9, 12–13, 14–16. Reprinted by permission of The Center for Shakespeare Studies.

[1] The present essay, in slightly different form, was delivered as a paper before the Shakespeare section of the Modern Language Association, at its annual convention, in New York, December, 1964.

[2] The New Variorum Edition of the play, ed. Matthias Shaaber (Philadelphia, 1940), pp. 584–99, provides plentiful examples of both views, but particularly of the second, or sentimentalist view, the moralistic position, in its fullest

Either of these formulations certainly oversimplifies, but my own instincts lead me to suspect that the latter view is the truer one, and that Bradley's essay still remains the soundest statement of the case. Bradley, it will be recalled, felt that the planned deterioration of Falstaff in *2 Henry IV,* carried out by Shakespeare with remarkable thoroughness, still could not prevail over the vitality intrinsic to the character (who embodies "the bliss of freedom gained in humour"); and that, conversely, the fact that the rejection is indeed necessary to the welfare of the kingdom, and the Prince has, in some sense, been rejecting Falstaff all along, could not dispel our feeling that the terms of the rejection are too peremptory and too scathing. . . .[3]

Prince Hal, like the king and courtiers in *Love's Labor's Lost,* has been on holiday, as he told us in his first soliloquy. Like the young lovers of *A Midsummer Night's Dream* he has been dreaming: he has "long dreamt of such a kind of man" (V.v.53). And it has been a dream of love: if the prince has not loved Falstaff, Falstaff has certainly loved the prince. As a symbol of "the supremacy of the imagination over fact," [4] Falstaff has glittered as enticingly as the moonlight in the Athens wood; as the incarnation of play, he has outstripped the young lords of Navarre even in their most inspired moments of sonneteering and masquerading. Following the lead of the comedies, then, we would expect the dream, the holiday, the moment of love, to have left some precious residue in the prince's spirit. We might suppose that certain human propensities were

development, being a more recent phenomenon. The Summer, 1956 (VII, #3), issue of *Shakespeare Quarterly,* a Supplement to the New Variorum Edition of *1 Henry IV,* ed. G. Blakemore Evans, contains a survey of later comment, in the Appendix, pp. 78–94. To the work of the two chief moralist critics, J. Dover Wilson and E. M. W. Tillyard, one may add such footnotes as Hugh Dickinson, "The Reformation of Prince Hal," *SQ,* XII (1951), 33–46, and Peter J. Seng, "Songs, Time, and the Rejection of Falstaff," *ShS,* XV (1962), 31–40.

[3] A. C. Bradley, "The Rejection of Falstaff," *Oxford Lectures on Poetry,* 2nd ed. (London, 1909), pp. 247–73. I should add that in addition to Bradley and Barber the critics who seem to me to have written most illuminatingly on Prince Hal and Falstaff are Harold C. Goddard, *The Meaning of Shakespeare* (Chicago, 1951), I, 167–213; Derek Traversi, *Shakespeare from Richard II to Henry V* (Stanford, 1957), pp. 162–65; and J. A. Bryant, Jr., "Prince Hal and the Ephesians," *Sewanee Review,* LXVII (1959), 204–19. The last-named essay, though it does not engage in debate with the moralist critics, constitutes one of the best rejoinders to them from a point of view explicitly Christian and theological. Goddard, II, 184–209, and Traversi, *An Approach to Shakespeare,* 2nd ed. (New York, 1956), pp. 235 ff., have also written penetratingly on the relations between love and power in *Antony and Cleopatra,* proposing a thesis essentially the same as that adopted in the final two paragraphs of the present essay. [See in this collection Bradley, pp. 71–77, and Traversi, pp. 99–102.]

[4] Harold C. Goddard, *The Meaning of Shakespeare* (Chicago, 1951), I, 179, 183.

better cultivated at Eastcheap than at court: the free pleasuring of the senses, the capacity to live in the present, undistracted by vain regrets over the past or empty wishes about the future, the love of wit and mirth, the invigorating skepticism toward received opinion and official rhetoric.

But unlike the heroes of the comedies, Hal is ashamed of his holiday, and he despises his dream. He recoils from his former lover with more of a shudder than Titania from the memory of Bottom. Nowhere does his final speech allow for the possibility that the sportive interlude was valuable. Where his counterparts in the comedies incorporate the holiday or the dream into their fuller waking lives, the new king dismisses it as a spell of "riot," a moment of worthless disorder. Instead of a synthesis, in which an enlarged sense of human possibility emerges from the dialectic between duty and holiday, or dream and waking, we have a forcible sundering of the two kinds of experience, and a walling of them off into the noncommunicating realms of Good and Bad.

The sundering is accompanied, inevitably, by a shrinking. Prince Hal is rightly said by Tillyard to be, in his tavern days, of a "comprehensive nature," responsive to the whole range of human potentiality. When he sounds the base string of humility in the company of the drawers, Hal is putting himself in vital touch with the whole spectrum of English life. He claims such a microcosmic comprehensiveness for himself when he announces that he is "of all humours that have showed themselves humours since the old days of goodman Adam" (*1H4*, II.iv.104–6). In Tillyard's gloss, he is claiming to be "ruled simultaneously by every human motive that exists." Now, his coronation accomplished, we find that he has cultivated this wide responsiveness only to disavow it and deliver homilies on it, that he is bent on rooting out of himself the variousness of feeling he once prided himself on—that, in short, his comprehensive nature is comprehensive no more, but partial and exclusive. . . .

"How ill white hairs become a fool and jester!" Folly, in Shakespeare, usually proves to be an inescapable condition of life, to which no one is immune, and jesters, to quote a perhaps not altogether trustworthy witness, "do oft prove prophets." Those who most fiercely claim exemption from folly are usually those suffering from hubris, for whom comic chastisement or tragic humbling is in store: the young men in *Love's Labor's Lost*, the fiery Lear. Acceptance of one's folly amounts to an acceptance of one's own earthy composition, and that of others: in both comic and tragic actions it forms an indispensable stage on the road to self-fulfillment. The newly crowned Henry V, by his categorical dismissal of folly, pursues the reverse course: he seeks to disclaim what he formerly acknowledged, his proneness to error, his membership in the race of goodman Adam. The rejection of Falstaff is part of a process in which, in the words of the Archbishop of Canterbury, "Consideration like an angel came/And whipp'd th'offending Adam out of him" (*H5*, I.i.28–29)—whereby the king disclaims the component of common clay in himself and sets himself apart from the stock of Adam. We are hardly surprised when later on, at the battlefield in France, he approves the execution of Bardolph without a flicker of recognition of the former association between them.

Now it is true that Hal is not the hero of a comedy, or of a tragedy, and that the experiences of romantic love, usually central to the comic formula, or of worldly ruin, central to tragedy, are here beside the point. It is true also that comic and tragic heroes ordinarily suffer from some defect of vision or error of feeling—Berowne's excessive penchant for mockery, Demetrius' whimsical fancy for Hermia—that must be corrected by whatever humbling experiences the plot affords. Hal, it may be argued, as the hero of a history play, suffers from no such defect. His task, according to the chief moralistic view, is not so much to understand himself, or to reform himself in any substantial way, as to fit himself to be the kind of king who will rule England wisely, and he is from the start in possession of his own best course. Eastcheap is not for him a regenerative wood, but a school of squalor where he learns plain truths about his future subjects and his realm. Even his most expansive moments, it may be urged, such as that with the drawers, are tinged with calculation; Hal is practising sounding the base string so as to be able later to play the whole gamut of the viol of state. But the more we insist on the element of planning in the Eastcheap truancy, the more we turn Hal into a cardboard prince, incapable from the outset of responding to the vitality of Falstaff. Under these conditions, the sojourn in the tavern becomes little better than an empty masquerade, and the gratuitous emphasis of the rejection speech seems more bizarre and inappropriate than ever. If, on the other hand, we grant the reality of the lure of Falstaff, as we surely experience it, and if we acknowledge what we plainly observe to be the case, that Falstaff delights the prince, then we find the exigencies of the history play leading to a "reformation" that we can only feel as a dehumanization.

Doubtless by progressively transforming revelry into misrule, during the latter scenes of *2 Henry IV*, Shakespeare has done what he could to justify dramatically the moralistic position. Having chosen to make Hal into the hero-king, a combination of both human and political virtues, he prepares the way for the crisis by making *us* reject Falstaff first. But those critics who have espoused the fierce tone as well as the dogma of the rejection scene have tended to give the episode a purely institutional reading. They have subscribed to the official doctrine according to which the prince makes himself the mirror of all Christian kings by disowning his past self. But Shakespearean characters do not achieve greatness by self-truncation, nor by adopting a priggish tone toward their own past misdeeds (if misdeeds they have committed). To banish plump Jack is to banish what is free and vital and pleasurable in life, as well as much that is selfish and unruly—not all the world perhaps, but more of it than either we or Hal can do without.

History thus defeats those who would defy it by trying to live in a changeless present or an undiminished youth, or in a realm of pure play. It awards its favors to those who can make themselves its servants by curbing their own human fullness. The history play as a genre—the Lancastrian tetralogy at least—takes an optimistic view of the process. It strives to present it as benign, so that the irresponsibles, who would flourish in comedy, are felt to deserve their defeat, while the exponents of order, however repressive, are felt to warrant our allegiance. In a later Shakespearean play a similar dilemma turns to tragedy. Antony and Cleopatra attempt to integrate into their public selves precisely the folly that Hal excludes from his: feasting, sensuality, music, sport, and idleness. In their case the spirit of the tavern is installed at the heart of their beings as monarchs; instead of being curbed and disciplined, it expands till it disables them as rulers. Their progress reverses Hal's: they start with business, empire, authority, the tyranny of time and the consciousness of limits, and end with play, sensuality, time transposed into eternity, and all limits obliterated and transcended. In their case holiday gradually invades the conduct of imperial business till it engrosses them utterly; the life of kingship gradually becomes the dream, the life of pleasure the engulfing, transcending reality. Where Hal fits himself as a ruler by scrapping part of his humanity, Antony and Cleopatra unfit themselves by fostering the totality of theirs. Only the Egyptian transvaluation by which things melt into and become each other's opposites permits them to translate their political failure into a spiritual victory.

This play too has tended to expose its readers as moralists and sentimentalists. Those who see in Falstaff chiefly a portent of disorder, to be rightly spurned by a repentant Hal come to his senses after a prodigal sowing of wild oats, also tend to see a cautionary tale in the story of Antony and Cleopatra, a homily against adultery and a warning against the neglect of serious business. Those who see in the sacrifice of Falstaff a near-tragic reproof of life by the tyrannical demands of state tend also to see in the deaths of Antony and Cleopatra a triumphant escape from the clutches of the same tyranny. In neither case, one suspects, can the conflicting forces be made to merge lastingly, or reach a stable equilibrium. Too many contradictory conditions exist to be satisfied. Life contains more than any given configuration in it can ever adequately embody, especially if that configuration straddles the public and private worlds as hugely as do the destinies of the English throne or the dynastic concerns of Egypt and ancient Rome. One must accept the fact that in one case political success is achieved at the cost of a constricted sensibility, in the other that a magnified sensibility is achieved at the price of imperial defeat.

PART TWO

View Points

Northrop Frye: Nature and Nothing

In the histories we notice the working of a principle that we might call Proust's law. The only paradises are the paradises we have lost, and every period of history seems to create a pastoral myth out of something in a previous age. The *Henry VI* plays naturally keep looking back to the days of Agincourt; but in the reigns of Henry IV and V too there are plots against the king that look back to the days of Richard as a kind of original social contract, all disasters being blamed on Bolingbroke's violation of this contract. We look back to the days of Richard, and find John of Gaunt taking the same view of the age of Edward III. In *Richard II* itself our sympathies are very evenly divided, because of the conception of nature involved. Richard, as king *de jure,* is the natural head of the state; because he does not do what is required of him in the state, society's natural need for order throws up another natural force in the form of Bolingbroke. Bolingbroke is neither a wicked usurper like Macbeth nor a righteous avenger like Hamlet, but, like Oliver Cromwell in Marvell's poem, a natural force that under certain conditions inevitably makes its appearance. His *de facto* authority, because of society's need of order, becomes *de jure* as well, a fact borne witness to by York's dramatic transfer of loyalties to him.

Still, the transfer of power from Richard to Bolingbroke does illustrate a breaking of the connection between human society and the cosmic order, and consequently the deposing of Richard creates a pastoral myth. As soon as Richard becomes impotent, all the magic of music and poetry becomes attached to him, aided by the fact that Richard is a poet himself. Once Henry IV is firmly established as king, he begins to bear the obloquy of responsibility, but neither his effort to dissociate himself from Richard's murder nor his dream of going on a crusade can give his crown the glamour that, in history, only a lost cause can have. Hotspur, with his tremendous

---

From "Nature and Nothing," by Northrop Frye. From Essays on Shakespeare, *ed. Gerald W. Chapman (Princeton, N.J.; Princeton University Press, 1965), pp. 42–44, 57–58. Copyright © 1965 by the Princeton University Press. Reprinted by permission of the publisher.*

energy and egoism, is very well adjusted to nature as an amoral
force, the aspect of nature that has been intensified by Henry's
accession. His contempt for poetry and music, however, indicates
that his instincts are for rebellion and anarchy rather than for order.
His much less likeable conqueror, Prince Henry, succeeds his
father legitimately, and so behaves like a *de jure* monarch, even to
the extent of describing the plot of Scroop and Grey against him as
"Another fall of man," echoing a phrase used by Queen Isabel in the
garden scene in *Richard II*. Despite the deep egoism that this phrase
suggests, Henry understands the conditions of royalty very well.
When his father dies and he is faced with two opposed symbolic
father-figures, the Chief Justice and Falstaff, he chooses the right
one and rejects the wrong one. His meditations about his father and
Richard just before Agincourt betray some uncertainty about his
claim to the English throne (to say nothing of the French one,
though France hardly counts in the argument), and perhaps some
in the audience might have remembered the poignant scene of the
death of Mortimer in *1 Henry VI*. Still, it is unnecessary for Henry
V to placate his God by building any more chantries for Richard,
because he is ascending the wheel of fortune, which does not start
turning downward until after his death. Only one phrase, in his
speech before Harfleur, "Disguise fair nature with hard-favoured
rage," shows any awareness on Henry's part that the level of nature
he represents is not the highest possible to man. This glimpse of a
better aspect of nature recurs in Burgundy's great speech on the
desolation of France already referred to, again in a context which
indicates its remoteness. In the world of present action, as Shakespeare presents it in the histories, there is a mixture of two things
that are separable when we think of them as past. One is the vision
of nature in its original human sense, the cosmic order forfeited by
the Fall, an event recalled by every act of treachery or usurpation
committed since. The other is nothingness, the abyss of annihilation
and nonbeing into which everything, so far as we can see, disappears.
Thus the revolving wheel of nature and fortune which is the
organizing principle of the histories contains a latent dialectic
expressed by the words "nature," in its upper-level sense, and
"nothing." . . .

. . . The dialectic of nature and nothing in Shakespeare turns
out to be also the dialectic of art and life, art being identical with
nature on its higher level, and guaranteeing, more clearly than any
myth of a lost paradise, a reality in our lives that is clear of the
dissolving chaos of experience.

Northrop Frye: Comedy and Falstaff

When Shakespeare began to study Plautus and Terence, his dramatic instinct, stimulated by his predecessors, divined that there was a profounder pattern in the argument of comedy than appears in either of them. At once—for the process is beginning in *The Comedy of Errors*—he started groping toward that profounder pattern, the ritual of death and revival that also underlines Aristophanes, of which an exact equivalent lay ready to hand in the drama of the green world. This parallelism largely accounts for the resemblances to Greek ritual which Colin Still has pointed out in *The Tempest.* . . .

The green world charges the comedies with a symbolism in which the comic resolution contains a suggestion of the old ritual pattern of the victory of summer over winter. This is explicit in *Love's Labor's Lost.* In this very masque-like play, the comic contest takes the form of the medieval debate of winter and spring. In *The Merry Wives of Windsor* there is an elaborate ritual of the defeat of winter, known to folklorists as "carrying out Death," of which Falstaff is the victim; and Falstaff must have felt that, after being thrown into the water, dressed up as a witch and beaten out of a house with curses, and finally supplied with a beast's head and singed with candles while he said, "Divide me like a brib'd buck, each a haunch," he had done about all that could reasonably be asked of any fertility spirit. . . .

The conception of a second world bursts the boundaries of Menandrine comedy, yet it is clear that the world of Puck is no world of eternal forms or divine revelation. Shakespeare's comedy is not Aristotelian and realistic like Menander's, nor Platonic and dialectic like Aristophanes', nor Thomist and sacramental like Dante's, but a fourth kind. It is an Elizabethan kind, and is not confined either to Shakespeare or to the drama. Spenser's epic is a wonderful contrapuntal intermingling of two orders of existence, one the red and white world of English history, the other the green world of the Faerie Queene. The latter is a world of crusading virtues proceeding from the Faerie Queene's court and designed to return to that court

"Comedy and Falstaff" [editor's title]. From "The Argument of Comedy," by Northrop Frye. From English Institute Essays, *1948, ed. D. A. Robertson, Jr. (New York: Columbia University Press), pp. 67, 68–69, 70–72, 72–73. Reprinted by permission of the publisher.*

when the destiny of the other world is fulfilled. The fact that the
Faerie Queene's knights are sent out during the twelve days of the
Christmas festival suggests our next point.

Shakespeare too has his green world of comedy and his red and
white world of history. The story of the latter is at one point interrupted by an invasion from the comic world, when Falstaff *senex et
parasitus* throws his gigantic shadow over Prince Henry, assuming
on one occasion the role of his father. Clearly, if the Prince is ever
to conquer France he must reassert the moral norm. The moral
norm is duly reasserted, but the rejection of Falstaff is not a comic
resolution. In comedy the moral norm is not morality but deliverance, and we certainly do not feel delivered from Falstaff as we feel
delivered from Shylock with his absurd and vicious bond. The moral
norm does not carry with it the vision of a free society: Falstaff will
always keep a bit of that in his tavern.

Falstaff is a mock king, a lord of misrule, and his tavern is a
Saturnalia. Yet we are reminded of the original meaning of the
Saturnalia, as a rite intended to recall the golden age of Saturn.
Falstaff's world is not a golden world, but as long as we remember it
we cannot forget that the world of *Henry V* is an iron one. We are
reminded too of another traditional denizen of the green world,
Robin Hood, the outlaw who manages to suggest a better kind of
society than those who make him an outlaw can produce. The out-
laws in *The Two Gentlemen of Verona* compare themselves, in
spite of the Italian setting, to Robin Hood, and in *As You Like It*
Charles the wrestler says of Duke Senior's followers: "There they
live like the old Robin Hood of England: they say many young
gentlemen flock to him every day, and fleet the time carelessly, as
they did in the golden world."

In the histories, therefore, the comic Saturnalia is a temporary
reversal of normal standards, comic "relief" as it is called, which
subsides and allows the history to continue. In the comedies, the
green world suggests an original golden age which the normal world
has usurped and which makes us wonder if it is not the normal
world that is the real Saturnalia. . . .

. . . We spend our lives partly in a waking world we call normal
and partly in a dream world which we create out of our own desires.
Shakespeare endows both worlds with equal imaginative power,
brings them opposite one another, and makes each world seem un-
real when seen by the light of the other. He uses freely both the
heroic triumph of New Comedy and the ritual resurrection of its
predecessor, but his distinctive comic resolution is different from
either: it is a detachment of the spirit born of this reciprocal re-

flection of two illusory realities. We need not ask whether this brings us into a higher order of existence or not, for the question of existence is not relevant to poetry.

We have spoken of New Comedy as Aristotelian, Old Comedy as Platonic and Dante's *commedia* as Thomist, but it is difficult to suggest a philosophical spokesman for the form of Shakespeare's comedy. For Shakespeare, the subject matter of poetry is not life, or nature, or reality, or revelation, or anything else that the philosopher builds on, but poetry itself, a verbal universe. That is one reason why he is both the most elusive and the most substantial of poets.

John F. Danby: Authority and Appetite

Hal, we have said, is Shakespeare's tired consciousness, Falstaff Shakespeare's unconscious. Hal is a polished Falconbridge: gay, courageous, patriotic, acquainted with every sort of man, the winner —in open competition—of all the social prizes; excellent in the taproom, on the battlefield, in the councils of state. There can be no doubt that he is intended for a new model King, a sixteenth-century paragon. The model itself, however, we have suggested, falls short of the absolute ideal Shakespeare has educated us already to expect. In the preceding chronicle plays the issues raised had been wider: Is the King right or wrong? Is the state just or unjust?—Even in the person of Jack Cade these questions are posed. In *Henry IV, Parts One and Two* the questions are reduced and vulgarized: Is the King strong or weak? Is the state secure or insecure? Shakespeare's first machiavel described the actual mechanics of human motive in society. Richard [III] appreciated the importance of self-interest, approved it, and decided on a ruthless employment of his intelligence to encompass the ends proposed by appetite. "Pity, love, and fear" he dismissed as irrelevancies. But Richard was wicked. Shakespeare insists that his choice was wrongful. Then the machiavel, and the society he interprets, is submitted to a process of whitewashing. This process ends in the machiavel of goodness, Prince Hal. Hal is no longer aware that society might be wicked. He espouses the aims and the means of the society to hand, he equips himself to be good in accordance with the terms of the State he will ultimately govern:

"*Authority and Appetite*" [*editor's title*]. From "*Edmund's Ancestry*," *by John F. Danby. From* Shakespeare's Doctrine of Nature: A Study of King Lear *(London: Faber & Faber, Ltd., 1949), pp. 90–92, 94–96, 97–98. Reprinted by permission of Faber & Faber, Ltd.*

Ile so offend, to make offence a skill.

This line gives the masterly essence of the new morality. Crude
machiavellism says that the end justifies the means. Refined machiavellism merely says: Let what you can do indicate what you can do
better: technique is the thing, let the ends look after themselves. It
is the attitude underlying sixteenth-century capitalist development
(in war, mining, and trade) and the attitude implied in the scientific
programmes which grew out of that development.

This twofold attitude to Hal involves a twofold attitude to Falstaff. In so far as we see Hal as the model chronicle-hero, in accordance with Shakespeare's intention, Falstaff will then be the decided
villain of the plays. If we tend to criticize Shakespeare's model as an
inadequate ideal, compared with his early chronicle plays and with
his later tragedies, then Falstaff will tend to acquire merit (deserved
or undeserved) from his rejection. Critics have followed both paths.
There has been a "Hal party" and a "Falstaff party." The point
missed in the debate has been, I think, the most important one:
that Falstaff and Hal belong together, that they can be accepted
together or rejected together. Shakespeare in *Henry IV* is a Shakespeare in transition. It is impossible to deny that he has already
moved on in the Hal plays themselves. And he is still moving. As
Hal turns away from Falstaff Shakespeare himself turns away from
Hal. . . .

The rejection of Falstaff by Hal is an allegory. Behind that allegory is the concrete world of Elizabeth and her England. The twin
forces in the sixteenth century state—each one needing the other,
both in an uneasy state of counterpoise, capable of clashing as well
as collaborating—were Appetite and Authority. In the rejection
scene Hal and my Lord Chief Justice stand for Authority; Falstaff
is Appetite, wonderfully enlarged, marvellously self-confident, a
"bolting hutch of beastliness," naïve and unashamed. Authority in
Elizabeth's world lived and was sustained by Appetite. It could not
have lasted in the world of Appetite, however, if it had not been
strong. Authority therefore was, in the end, Power. Power was
needed in the Tudor world (as in Henry V's) to centralize, organize, canalize, concentrate, and sometimes curb Appetite; to check
it and give it more adequate goals—Spanish treasure fleets instead
of merchant men on Gadshill, the Grand Lease of the Prince
Bishop's coal mines instead of Mistress Quickly's bed linen. Falstaff's
world is a symbol of the unofficial side of Elizabeth's reign. There
was always also the official sphere of order and ceremony and
decorum the buccaneer and entrepreneur readily fell in with. But

the real work of the realm was done on the high seas by the bucca-
neers, in the coal mines and salt-beds and glass and brass manufac-
tories by the entrepreneur: an unofficial realm Elizabeth could only
recognize in private, when the attention of the rest of Europe was
distracted elsewhere.

The high life of Elizabeth's monopolist-courtiers we see in *Henry
IV, Part One,* when Hotspur and Glendower are quarrelling over
the carving-up of the Kingdom. The unvarnished version is Falstaff
and his retainers at their shady business. Appetite monstrous and
unabashed, as plausible as it is unlimited, strides through London
and the English countryside in Falstaff's person. The protective
camouflage of the official world he does not need. His cynicism, as
Bradley points out, pierces to the bottom of truth, honour, law,
patriotism, duty, courage, war, religion. And everything at bottom,
he sees—as the machiavel does—is self-preservation: "What, ye
rogues, young men must live." His is the vitality and conscienceless-
ness of Hawkins on the high seas. Hal, as Authority, is Elizabeth.
Elizabeth had her unruly brigandage which nourished, supported,
and sometimes clumsily clashed with her "Order"—Drakes who
flouted her with her silent permission, Essexes who presumed too
far on the strength of the Queen's favour and met with sudden re-
buff. Hal throws off Falstaff in order to be a more effective King:
Elizabeth put away the flesh to be all the more effectively the Virgin
Queen. Elizabeth's asceticism, of course, had its limits. Love of
pomp, display, flattery, and money she indulged to the full. Hal's
moral stance also has its limits, the limits of the necessity to be
strong in possession of his throne, and the original limits of his
entire manoeuvre to make reformation a means rather than an
end. . . .

Analysis leaves us, then, with symbols of Power and Appetite as
the keys to the plays meaning: Power and Appetite, the two sides of
Commodity. The world is disunited and corrupt at heart. Corruption and disunity spread, too, through the whole body politic. The
England depicted in *Henry IV, Parts One and Two* is neither ideally
ordered nor happy. It is an England, on the one side, of bawdy-
house and thieves'-kitchen, of waylaid merchants, badgered and
bewildered Justices, and a peasantry wretched, betrayed, and recruited for the wars; an England, on the other side, of the chivalrous
wolf-pack of Hotspur and Douglas, and of state-sponsored treachery
in the person of Prince John—the whole presided over by a sick
King, hagridden by conscience, dreaming of a Crusade to the Holy
Land as M. Remorse thinks of slimming and repentance. Those who
see the world of *Henry IV* as some vital, joyous Renaissance England

must go behind the facts Shakespeare presents. It is a world where to be normal is to be anti-social, and to be social is to be anti-human. Humanity is split in two. One half is banished to an underworld where dignity and decency must inevitably submerge in brutality and riot. The other half is restricted to an over-world where the same dignity and decency succumb to heartlessness and frigidity.

Harold Jenkins: The Structural Problem in Shakespeare's *Henry the Fourth*

. . . I hold it reasonable to infer from the analysis I have given that in the course of writing *Henry IV* Shakespeare changed his mind. I am compelled to believe that the author himself foresaw, I will even say intended, that pattern which evolves through the early acts of Part One and which demands for its completion that the hero's rise to an eminence of valour shall be accomplished, or at least swiftly followed, by the banishment of the riotous friends who hope to profit from his reign. In other words, hard upon the Battle of Shrewsbury there was to come the coronation of the hero as king. This inference from the play is not without support from other evidence. The prince's penitence in the interview with his father in the middle of Part One corresponds to an episode which, both in Holinshed and in the play of *The Famous Victories of Henry the Fifth,* is placed only shortly before the old king's death. And still more remarkable is the sequence of events in a poem which has been shown to be one of Shakespeare's sources.[1] At the historical Battle of Shrewsbury the Prince was only sixteen years old, whereas Hotspur was thirty-nine. But in Samuel Daniel's poem, *The Civil Wars,* Hotspur is made "young" and "rash" and encounters a prince of equal age who emerges like a "new-appearing glorious star." [2] It is Daniel, that is to say, who sets in opposition these two splendid youths and so provides the germ from which grows the rivalry of the Prince and Hotspur which is structural to Shakespeare's play. And in view of this resemblance between Daniel and Shakespeare, it is significant that Daniel ignores the ten years that in history

From The Structural Problem in Shakespeare's *Henry the Fourth, by Harold Jenkins (London: Methuen & Co., Ltd., 1956), pp. 19–23, 25–27. Copyright © 1956 by Methuen & Co., Ltd. Reprinted by permission of the publisher.*

[1] See F. W. Moorman, "Shakespeare's History Plays and Daniel's 'Civil Wars,'" *Shakespeare Jahrbuch,* XL (1904), 77–83.

[2] Book III, stanzas 97, 109–10.

elapsed between the death of Hotspur and the Prince's accession. Whereas in Holinshed the events of those ten years fill nearly twenty pages, Daniel goes straight from Shrewsbury to the old king's death-bed. This telescoping of events, which confronts the Prince with his kingly responsibilities directly after the slaying of Hotspur, adumbrates the pattern that Shakespeare, as I see it, must have had it in mind to follow out. The progress of a prince was to be presented not in two phases but in a single play of normal length which would show the hero wayward in its first half, pledging reform in the middle, and then in the second half climbing at Shrewsbury the ladder of honour by which, appropriately, he would ascend to the throne.

The exact point at which a new pattern supervenes I should not care to define. But I think the new pattern can be seen emerging during the fourth act. At a corresponding stage the history play of *Richard II* shows the deposition of its king, *Henry V* the victory at Agincourt, even *Henry IV* Part Two the quelling of its rebellion in Gaultree Forest. By contrast *Henry IV* Part One, postponing any such decisive action, is content with preparation. While the rebels gather, the Prince is arming and Falstaff recruiting to meet them. Until well into the fifth act ambassadors are going back and forth between the rival camps, and we may even hear a message twice over, once when it is despatched and once when it is delivered. True, this is not undramatic: these scenes achieve a fine animation and suspense as well as the lowlier feat of verisimilitude. But the technique is obviously not one of compression. Any thought of crowding into the two-hour traffic of one play the death of the old king and the coronation of the new has by now been relinquished, and instead the Battle of Shrewsbury is being built up into a grand finale in its own right. In our eagerness to come to this battle and our gratification at the exciting climax it provides, we easily lose sight of our previous expectations. Most of us, I suspect, go from the theatre well satisfied with the improvised conclusion. It is not, of course, that we cease to care about the fate of individuals. On the contrary, the battle succeeds so well because amid the crowded tumult of the fighting it keeps the key figures in due prominence. Clearly showing who is killed, who is rescued, and who shams dead, who slays a valiant foe and who only pretends to, it brings each man to a destiny that we perceive to be appropriate. We merely fail to notice that the destiny is not in every case exactly what was promised. There is no room now in Part One to banish Falstaff. A superb comic tact permits him instead the fate of reformation, in fact the alternative of giving over instead of being damned. It is a

melancholy fate enough, for it means giving over being Falstaff:
we leave him saying that if he is rewarded, he will "leave sack, and
live cleanly as a nobleman should do." But since this resolution is
conditional and need in any case be believed no more than Falstaff
has already taught us to believe him, it has the advantage that it
leaves the issue open, which, to judge from the outcry there has
always been over the ending of Part Two, is how most people would
prefer to have it left. Shakespeare's brilliant improvisation thus
provides a dénouement to Part One which has proved perfectly ac-
ceptable, while it still leaves opportunity for what I hope I may call
the original ending, if the dramatist should choose to add a second
part. I refrain, however, from assuming that a second part was
necessarily planned before Part One was acted. . . . In the two parts
of *Henry IV* there are not two princely reformations but two versions of a single reformation. And they are mutually exclusive.
Though Part Two frequently recalls and sometimes depends on
what has happened in Part One, it also denies that Part One exists.
Accordingly the ideal spectator of either part must not cry with
Shakespeare's Lucio, "I know what I know." He must sometimes
remember what he knows and sometimes be content to forget it.
This, however, is a requirement made in some degree by any work
of fiction, or as they used to call it, feigning. And the feat is not a
difficult one for those accustomed to grant the poet's demand for
"that willing suspension of disbelief . . . which constitutes poetic
faith."

Henry IV, then, is both one play and two. Part One begins an
action which it finds it has not scope for but which Part Two rounds
off. But with one half of the action already concluded in Part One,
there is danger of a gap in Part Two. To stop the gap Part Two
expands the unfinished story of Falstaff and reduplicates what is
already finished in the story of the Prince. The two parts are complementary, they are also independent and even incompatible. What
they are, with their various formal anomalies, I suppose them to
have become through what Johnson termed "the necessity of ex-
hibition." Though it would be dangerous to dispute Coleridge's
view that a work of art must "contain in itself the reason why it is
so," that its form must proceed from within,[3] yet even works of art,

---

[3] This is a synthesis of several passages in Coleridge. The words in quotation
marks are said of whatever can give permanent pleasure; but the context shows
Coleridge to be thinking of literary composition. See *Biographia Literaria*, ed.
Shawcross, ii. 9. Also relevant are "On Poesy or Art," *ibid*, ii. 262; and *Coleridge's
Shakespearean Criticism,* ed. T. M. Raysor, i. 223–24.

like other of man's productions, must submit to the bondage of the finite. . . .

Derek Traversi: The Climax of the Play

With the entry of Hotspur, the central duel between rival conceptions of "honour" and their relation to the "destiny" which overshadows them is at last brought to a head. These conceptions are, indeed, mutually exclusive; this is implied in the Prince's words "Two stars keep not their motion in one sphere," and the type of "glory" with which both are here concerned is not of the kind that can be shared in life. The clash between them follows, and as a result of it Hotspur dies. His last speech is important in its suggestion of a relationship between the speaker's conception of "honour," now tragically affirmed in death, and certain themes simultaneously growing to mature expression in Shakespeare's work at this same period. Hotspur, dying, affirms the value of the "proud titles" of glory above that of "brittle life"; but in the adjective there is a sense of hollowness, of disillusionment, which contrasts with the content of the vaguely conceived "titles" themselves and suggests, most typically, that sense of tragic emptiness which Shakespeare, from this time, comes increasingly to set in pathetic contrast to the heroic ideal. The whole of Hotspur's final utterance is wrapped in a characteristic pessimism:

> They wound my thoughts worse than thy sword my flesh:
> But thought's the slave of life, and life time's fool;
> And time, that takes survey of all the world,
> Must have a stop.   (V.iv)

To interpret this speech adequately is to be aware of a conflict more subtle than may immediately appear. It is, indeed, at once an attempted excuse for inner emptiness, for chivalrous values seen at the decisive moment to be void of true significance, and a pathetic affirmation of the tragedy which the recognition of this emptiness implies. The sense of the passage of time, unredeemed by a corresponding conception of "value," is typical of many of the sonnets

---

and of much of Shakespeare's work at this period. Originally
relatively abstract in expression, we see it now in the process of
acquiring a personal and pathetic quality which will eventually
affect the dramatist's attitude to his tragic heroes.

At this point, indeed, Hotspur is at once expressing disillusionment and, in expressing it, seeking a certain emotional compensa-
tion. His disillusionment, moreover, needs to be seen in relation to
the action in which he has allowed his shallow, if true, generosity,
to be involved. At Shrewsbury, he has fallen before a conception of
"honour" at once deeper and, as the future will confirm, more
efficient than his own; but he has fallen also on behalf of the policies
incarnated in Worcester, policies which his emotion has too readily
accepted but which are less creditable than those which his own
nature should have been capable of assimilating. Hotspur's death
leaves us with an impression poised between the tragic and the
ironic, adequately summed up in the self-conscious pathos of his
reference to the "earthy and cold hand of death" and in the contrast of attitudes contained in his conqueror's brief completion of
his final "food for—": "For *worms, brave* Percy." This is simply
one aspect of the fatality that overshadows a battle in which the
rebels fail to attain their end and in which it is foreseen that the
king will equally be prevented from achieving the unity for which
he is *now*, but too late, genuinely striving.

The Prince's oration over his dead rival is, as far as it goes, fitting
and impressive; but it belongs, like so much in his nature, to the
public rather than to the truly personal order. In calling Hotspur
"great heart" and "so stout a gentleman" he affirms the values of
courtesy which are to be a necessary part of his own developing
royal virtues; but, even in so doing, in the lending of his "favours"
to cover his former enemy's "mangled face" with "rites of tender-
ness," we feel a weight correspondingly laid on vanity:

> When that this body did contain a spirit,
> A kingdom for it was too small a bound;
> But now two paces of the vilest earth
> Is room enough.   (V.iv)

Beneath the formal quality of this "epitaph," giving personal content to the conventional gesture, lies a preoccupation with "igno-
miny" and with the "vanity" upon which, as we have seen, Falstaff
has already touched in irony; the modification of the chivalrous note
by a qualifying sense of tragedy is full of meaning for the interpretation of the spirit of later plays.

It is no accident that Falstaff has been present as a spectator at
this culminating moment in the duel of contrasted conceptions of
"honour." Before the battle, his contact with the popular sphere
represented a parallel, at once cynical and truly humourous, to the
"serious" action, and now his mock death at the hands of Douglas
carries this parallel to a logical culmination; whilst the Prince,
having delivered his chivalrous epitaph over Hotspur, turns to a
comic shadow of it in his reflections over Falstaff's body:

> O, I should have a heavy miss of thee,
> If I were much in love with vanity!
> Death hath not struck so fat a deer to-day,
> Though many dearer, in this bloody fray.   (V.iv)

The easy flow of rhyme offers a clear contrast to the preceding
heroic seriousness in blank verse, and even the reference to "vanity"
rouses echoes from the past action. The Prince's own humour, with
its self-conscious disclaimer "If I were much in love with vanity,"
is indeed in character, as is the spirit of the pun on "deer" and
"dearer" which can be paralleled elsewhere in his utterances. Comic
as the speech is in intention—lest we should be tempted to take
Falstaff too seriously, a fault not always successfully avoided—its
spirit is that of a commentary offered in character, a placing of
what has gone before; nor is this mock death, and the Prince's
equally mock farewell, at this moment in which he has decisively
confirmed himself in his "serious," political function, entirely without significance for their future relationship.

Falstaff's following comment, after his "resurrection," contains as
usual an assertion of life, of simple vitality, against the claims of
verbal obligation: "To die, is to be a counterfeit; for he is but the
counterfeit of a man who hath not the life of a man: but to counterfeit dying, when a man thereby liveth, is to be no counterfeit, but
the true and perfect image of life indeed." In the light of this assertion, the speaker's "cowardice" is seen to include a positive comic
value, and even the final stabbing of Hotspur's dead body and the
taking of the grotesque burden on to his back, though no doubt it
is the final manifestation of the predatory tradition of the braggart
soldier of theatrical convention, contains also an ironic reference to
the serious, "chivalrous" combat we have just witnessed. Equally,
the very monstrous manner in which he claims his reward before
the Prince—"I look to be either earl or duke, I can assure you"—is
inspired not only by the hope of advancement but by an ironic
attitude to the courtly dignities mentioned, in a similarly comic
spirit, in his last words in this play: "He that rewards me, God re-

ward him! If I do grow great, I'll grow less; for I'll purge, and leave
sack, and live cleanly as a nobleman should do." The mock reference to emendation, the last of several in *Henry IV,* Part One, need
not be taken solely, as some students of the play have taken it, as an
anticipation of the advances obtained by Falstaff as a result of his
fictitious exploit. It is true that Falstaff will appear, in the following
play, with a new range of monstrous social pretensions. To that
extent, these concluding words look forward to what we shall see to
be the changed spirit of Part Two; but here its counterpart is the
Prince's priggish (surely not "generous," as some have held it to be)
and contemptuous comment:

> For my part, if a lie may do thee grace,
> I'll gild it with the happiest terms I have,

and its value is eminently satirical.

Robert Langbaum: Character versus Action in Shakespeare

The issue between the psychological and anti-psychological interpretations of Falstaff is whether as coward, lecher and glutton he
is the butt of the comedy and deservedly outwitted in the end; or
whether he is the maker of the comedy, playing the butt for the sake
of the humour which he turns upon himself as well as everyone
else—whether he is, in other words, victorious in all the wit combats
whatever his circumstantial defeat. It is essentially the issue of Hamlet and Macbeth criticism, whether they confront their difficulties or
create them; and of Iago criticism, whether he is the villain or as
maker of the plot merely playing the villain. In other words, are
the characters agents of the plot with only as much consciousness as
the plot requires; or have they a residue of intelligence and will
beyond what the plot requires and not accounted for by it, so that
they stand somehow above the plot, conscious of themselves inside
it? The latter view assumes that we can apprehend more about the
characters than the plot tells us, assumes our sympathetic apprehension of them.

From *"Character versus Action in Shakespeare,"* by Robert Langbaum. From
The Poetry of Experience (*New York: Random House, Inc., 1957; London:
Chatto & Windus, Ltd., 1957*), *pp. 170–71, 176–78, 179–80. Copyright © 1957 by
Robert Langbaum. Reprinted by permission of the publishers.*

The Falstaff question has been only less important than the Hamlet question in establishing the psychological interpretation of Shakespeare. Both Hamlet and Falstaff began to appear in their new complex and enigmatic character in the 1770's, the decade of Werther and of a European Wertherism that owed much to an already well-established sentimental tradition in England. Of such a propitious age for psychological criticism, Maurice Morgann, the projector of the new Falstaff, was one of the advanced spirits—liberal in politics, humanitarian in sentiment, and in literature endowed with the new sensibility. . . . The attack on prudence is the beginning of the romantic ethics. Hypocrisy (the denial of one's own nature) is its worst sin, sincerity (another name for existential courage) its prime virtue. Morgann's Falstaff has the virtues Blake was to recommend in *The Marriage of Heaven and Hell:* "Prudence is a rich, ugly old maid courted by Incapacity," "He who desires but acts not, breeds pestilence," "The road of excess leads to the palace of wisdom." *Excess* explains Falstaff's nature; his girth, his appetites, his laughter, even his style of wit and the rich redundancy of his language—all derive their character from excess; yet they are not for that reason vices, as they would be according to the Aristotelian ethics of the Golden Mean. According to the new ethics, Falstaff's excesses are at once the cause of his failure and of his distinction.

For he commits what Shelley was to call the "generous error," the error of those who try to live life by a vision of it, thus transforming the world about them and impressing upon it their character. This is the secret of Falstaff's appeal. His vision of life takes over whenever he is on the stage; and everyone on stage with him, most notably the Prince, is drawn into his characteristic atmosphere. The only characters who resist his influence are those who, like the King and Hotspur, never confront him. Yet Falstaff's genius for creating his own environment is dangerous, since the single vision of life cannot be identical with reality and must eventually collide with it. That is why the "generous error" distinguishes the Hero of Existence from what Shelley calls the "trembling throng," who "languish" and are "morally dead," who live eclectically because they have not the courage to live out the implications of their own natures, who are too prudent to venture all on what must turn out to have been a noble delusion.[1]

Dr. Johnson, who saw where Morgann's kind of criticism was leading, said of him: "Why, Sir, we shall have the man come forth again; and as he has proved Falstaff to be no coward, he may prove

---

[1] See the Preface to *Alastor* and the last stanza of *Adonais*.

Iago to be a very good character." [2] Johnson thought he was indulging in witty hyperbole, but the admiration for Falstaff was in
fact to be accompanied in the next century by an admiration for
Iago and for all characters alive enough to take over the scene, to
assert their point of view as the one through which we understand
the action. The new existential rather than moral judgment of
character was to dissolve dramatic structure by denying the authority of the plot—making the psychologically read play, like the
dramatic monologue, depend for its success upon a central character
with a point of view definite enough to give meaning and unity
to the events, and the strength of intellect, will and passion, the
imaginative strength, to create the whole work before our eyes, to
give it a thickness and an atmosphere, in inner momentum, a life.

It is, however, in the isolation of character from plot that we can
best see the psychological interpretation of Shakespeare as dissolving
dramatic structure and leading us toward the dramatic monologue.
For in concentrating on the part of character in excess of plot requirements, and in claiming to apprehend more about character
than the plot reveals, the psychological interpretation isolates
character from the external motivation of plot (such as money, love,
power). It makes of character an autonomous force, motivated solely
by the need for self-expression. The psychological interpretation of
Falstaff rests, for example, on the assumption that Falstaff does not
employ his wit for practical advantage, that he makes no secret of
his true nature and therefore does not really expect to deceive the
other characters but merely to draw them into his jests. Deny this
assumption as Stoll does, and you have a Falstaff who menaces the
other characters and vies for advantage in the same way as the rival
factions of the play's historical episodes. Such a Falstaff must be
judged morally and laughed at as a base clown who is deservedly
humiliated and outwitted at every turn. [3]

But Morgann's Falstaff employs his wit not as the "instrument of
power" but as "power itself." And Hazlitt's Falstaff is less interested
in sensual gratification than in his own "ideal exaggerated descrip-
tion" of the life of sensuality and freedom, of a world-view he has
taken it upon himself to dramatize.

> His pulling out the bottle in the field of battle is a joke to shew his
> contempt for glory accompanied with danger, his systematic adherence

[2] James Boswell, *The Life of Samuel Johnson, LL.D.* (London: J. M. Dent,
1901), III, 230.

[3] [See E. E. Stoll, *Shakespeare Studies* (New York, 1927).]

to his Epicurean philosophy in the most trying circumstances. Again, such is his deliberate exaggeration of his own vices, that it does not seem quite certain whether the account of his hostess's bill, found in his pocket, with such an out-of-the-way charge for capons and sack with only one halfpennyworth of bread, was not put there by himself as a trick to humour the jest upon his favourite propensities, and as a conscious caricature of himself. He is represented as a liar, a braggart, a coward, a glutton, &c. and yet we are not offended but delighted with him; for he is all these as much to amuse others as to gratify himself. He openly assumes all these characters to shew the humorous part of them. . . . In a word, he is an actor in himself almost as much as upon the stage, and we no more object to the character of Falstaff in a moral point of view than we should think of bringing an excellent comedian, who should represent him to the life, before one of the police offices.[4]

Falstaff has no motive other than to exercise his genius for comedy. . . .

The effectiveness of character is made to depend on its inaccessibility to the rational and moral categories of the plot. Falstaff, Hamlet, and Iago are geniuses whose only purpose is to express their genius. They are creators of the play who must be judged not as we judge men of action but as we judge artists, by the virtuosity of their creations. It matters less whether they are right than that they accomplish what they set out to be and do—that Falstaff conquer with his wit, that Hamlet gain spiritual ascendancy through his moving and profound exploration of moral experience, and that Iago's intrigue be bold, ingenious and successful.

Such a theory is in its ultimate implication destructive of drama. It destroys the play as an entity distinct from its parts, having a logic, meaning, and unity of its own to which the parts are subordinated; for it destroys the objective principles which relate the events and characters to each other and to the whole. By leaving events subject to the will of character, it destroys the logic inherent in the events themselves. And by giving unconditional sympathy to sheer vividness of character, it destroys the moral principle which apportions sympathy among the characters according to their deserts. It leaves an anarchic free-for-all in which the characters compete for a sympathy that depends on the ability to command attention, with the strongest character able to assert his point of view against the general meaning.

[4] *Characters of Shakespear's Plays,* pp. 190–91.

Norman Rabkin: Life and Power in the Histories

In one respect *Richard II* sets the terms for all the political plays Shakespeare will write after it: political success, defined in whatever terms the play's situation requires, will always be complementary to qualities of the human spirit incompatible with it. Shakespeare does not scorn such success—the harmonious commonwealth is an ideal he teaches us to value as few other writers do—but he makes us fully aware of the cost of achieving it. In the two plays that deal with the later fortunes of Henry IV Shakespeare frames the question of the value of political success in terms to which he will return with less optimism in *Antony and Cleopatra,* setting political responsibility against all that Falstaff represents. To call it hedonism is to make a judgment on it to which the play calls us more than once as the fat knight's constitutional inability and willful refusal to think in terms of his obligations come into conflict with what the patriotic ambiance and Hal's plight demand. But though he is a liar, Falstaff never misrepresents himself as a patriot, and even when we are angry at him for his monumental irresponsibility in raising troops, we can never reproach him for hypocrisy. Falstaff conveys the sense of life, sensual and unpurposive, life at any cost, life as the most absolute of values, in whose way no obstacle must be allowed to stand. His funniest moments invariably fill us with the joy of recognizing his preposterous insistence on remaining young despite his considerable age ("Young men must live"), on playing holiday like a truant schoolboy all year long, on cheating death with indefatigable vigor and inventiveness; his most poignant moments invariably remind us that he grows old, that finally death may make the claim on him that in life a sense of responsibility could not.

Yet for all that he must be rejected, in favor of an understanding of the world which allows little room for the spirit of perpetual play that Falstaff embodies. To be Falstaff one must turn away from the world of time, cease considering oneself as a participant in history. "What a devil hast thou to do with the time of the day?" asks Hal in his first speech to Sir John:

"Life and Power in the Histories" [*editor's title*]. *From "The Polity," by Norman Rabkin. From* Shakespeare and the Common Understanding (*New York: The Free Press, 1967*), *pp. 95–97, 100–101. Copyright © 1967 by the Free Press, a division of Macmillan Company. Reprinted by permission of the publisher.*

Unless hours were cups of sack and minutes capons and clocks the
tongues of bawds and dials the signs of leaping-houses and the blessed
sun himself a fair hot wench in flame-coloured taffeta, I see no reason
why thou shouldst be so superfluous to demand the time of day.

(I.ii.7–13)

But at the moment of his finest self-knowledge, Richard has already
acknowledged that playing Falstaff's game in the world of men has
been his undoing and England's:

> Music do I hear?
> Ha, ha! keep time: how sour sweet music is,
> When time is broke and no proportion kept!
> So is it in the music of men's lives.
> And here have I the daintiness of ear
> To check time broke in a disorder'd string;
> But for the concord of my state and time
> Had not an ear to hear my true time broke.
> I wasted time, and now doth time waste me. . . .
>
> (*Richard II*, V.v.41–49)

Hal tells us in his first soliloquy that he is a man who knows time
and therefore will ultimately redeem it, that all the year is not
playing holiday, and he shares his father's skill in judging the propitious time for the conduct of affairs. What he knows is what
Shakespeare tells us over and over: The movement of history has
its own inexorable logic, and its medium is time. To succeed one
must be able to seize the moment, to think always in terms of time.
In *Troilus and Cressida* and *Othello* we [find] passages, spoken by
characters as different as Ulysses and Iago, in which time is described
as if it were an autonomous organism; and such a passage we find
at a crucial and retrospective moment in the Henriad, as Henry IV
ruefully recalls Richard's prophecy that a time would come when the
coalition supporting the new king would break apart. His friend
the Duke of Warwick answers him in words that might be a motto
for the entire tetralogy:

> There is a history in all men's lives,
> Figuring the natures of the times deceased;
> The which observed, a man may prophesy,
> With a near aim, of the main chance of things
> As yet not come to life, which in their seeds
> And weak beginnings lie intreasured.
> Such things become the hatch and brood of time;

And by the necessary form of this
King Richard might create a perfect guess
That great Northumberland, then false to him,
Would of that seed grow to a greater falseness;
Which should not find a ground to root upon,
Unless on you.   (2 *Henry IV,* III.i.80–92)

No more a mystic than Shakespeare, Warwick roots the inevi-
tability of the history he describes in the natures of the men involved in it. But given that point of view, what we love in Falstaff
is no alternative to political commitment, and Hal has no choice but
to reject it. On the other hand, Shakespeare presents Flagstaff so that
we do love him, and by setting against him, with his catechistic
demolition of honor, a Hotspur who carries the belief in honor to
extremes that show its ultimate meaninglessness, by setting Hal
symbolically and actually on the stage between the dead Hotspur
and Falstaff risen from his mock death, and by making us recognize
the unexpected inadequacy of Henry IV and the uneasy compromise
built into the life of his perplexing son, Shakespeare suggests to us
once again in the *Henry IV* plays the welter of emotions with which
we contemplate history, committed and detached, hopeful and des-
pairing, sure that politics can and must save us and at the same
time contemptuously certain that it is irrelevant to our realest
lives. . . .

The problem common to the four plays of Shakespeare's second
cycle of history plays can thus be seen to arise from a view of man's
tragic nature much like that of the psychoanalysts: Man is tragically
torn between on the one hand the ethical demands made on him by
his role in history and by that part of his personality which is compelled to accede to such demands, and on the other the instinctive
sense that life is an amoral and absolute end in itself, and that only
that matters which brings gratification to all the animal instincts,
including the impulse to play. As we have seen, Shakespeare makes
it finally impossible for his audience to choose the pleasure principle or the reality principle as the single basis of the good life, and
he is no more optimistic than Freud about the possibility of living
in a balance between the two. A version of the general dichotomy we
have been observing in plays that deal with other problems, the
view of human nature developed in the history plays reminds us
that the roots of Shakespeare's psychology and ethics are planted in
the neoplatonic and Christian tradition which sees man as an uneasy
amalgam of opposed elements, soul and body, angel and beast.
But unlike neoplatonists and Christians, Shakespeare does not resolve

this problematic dichotomy by a resolution in favor of what tradition saw as the superior element in human nature, and this is why modern readers rightly recognize that his affinities are as much with the psychoanalytic as with the Christian understanding.

Ernst Kris: Prince Hal's Conflict

The conflict between father and son appears in Part One of Henry IV in three versions, each time enacted by one central and two related characters.[1] The theme is manifestly stated by the King in the introductory scene of the trilogy, when he compares Henry of Monmouth to Henry Percy. . . .

The position of the Prince between Falstaff and the King is almost as explicitly stated; he has two fathers, as the King has two sons. When he enacts with Falstaff his forthcoming interview with his father, the theme is brought into the open.[2] It is not limited to court and tavern, the centers of the "double plot," as W. Empson (1935) calls it, but extends to the rebel camp. Henry Percy stands between a weak father, Northumberland, who is prevented by illness from participating in the decisive battle, and a scheming uncle, Worcester, who plans the rebellion, conceals from Percy that the King offers reconciliation and drives him thus to battle and to death.

The three versions of the father-son conflict compelled Shakespeare to deviate from his sources and thereby to enrich the stage: he sharpened the report of the chronicles on the rebellion of the Percies in order to create the contrast of Worcester and Northumberland; he reduced Henry Percy's age from a slightly older contemporary of Henry IV to a somewhat older contemporary of the Prince—and he invented Falstaff.

The triangular relationships are not only similar to each other, since they all contain variations of the theme of good and bad fathers and sons, but within each triangle the parallel figures are closely interconnected; thus the two Harrys, whom Henry IV com-

---

From "Prince Hal's Conflict," by Ernst Kris. From The Psychoanalytic Quarterly, *XVII* (October, *1948*), *492, 493–94, 498–99, 502–503, 504.* Copyright © *1948* by The Psychoanalytic Quarterly. *Reprinted by permission of the publisher.*

[1] That the repetition of one theme in various configurations indicates its central position was pointed out by Jekels (1933).

[2] The idea of the travestied interview itself is borrowed from *The Famous Victories of Henry the Fifth.* There the Prince and his companions enact the Prince's subsequent interview with the Chief Justice.

pares, form a unit; Hotspur's rebellion represents also Prince Hal's unconscious parricidal impulses.[3] Hotspur is the Prince's double. Impulses pertaining to one situation have thus been divided between two personages,[4] but though in the triangles the characters are paired and contrasted, each of the play's personages transcends the bondage to his function in this thematic configuration. They have all outgrown the symmetry which they serve, into the fullness of life. . . .

. . . The Prince tries to dissociate himself from the crime his father had committed; he avoids contamination with regicide because the impulse to regicide (parricide) is alive in his unconscious. When the King's life is threatened he saves the King and kills the adversary, who is his alter ego. In shunning the court for the tavern he expresses his hostility to his father and escapes the temptation to parricide. He can permit himself to share Falstaff's vices because he does not condone the King's crime; but hostility to the father is only temporarily repressed. When finally he is in possession of the crown, he turns against the father substitute; hence the pointed cruelty of Falstaff's rejection. Both paternal figures between which the Prince oscillates have less meaning to him than appears at first. What he opposes to them is different and of an exalted nature: his ideals of kingship, royal duty and chivalry. These ideals are with him when he first appears on the stage; they grow in and with him throughout the tragedy, and they dominate throughout the five acts of *King Henry V*.

These ideals, one might speculate, may have been modeled on an idealization of Richard II, the murdered King, whom Prince Hal as a boy had accompanied to Ireland and whose favor he had won. . . .

Hamlet stands between a murdered father and a murderous uncle. Prince Hal's father murdered his second cousin—and predecessor—to whom the Prince had an attachment. Thus the crime is in both cases carried out by the father or by his substitute—the King in Hamlet—while both heroes are battling against the murderous impulse in their own hearts.

The psychological plausibility of Prince Hal as a dramatic character is not inferior to that of Hamlet, whatever the difference in depth and dramatic significance of the two plays may be. While only one part of the oedipal conflict is presented, the defenses which Prince Hal mobilizes in order to escape from his internal

[3] This point was made by Alexander (1933), and by Empson [*Some Versions of Pastoral*] (1935, p. 43).

[4] Ernest Jones (1911, 1949) speaks in a similar connection of decomposition.

predicament are well known from the clinical study of male youths. In our analysis of the Prince's character we have implicitly referred mainly to two mechanisms: first, to the formation of the superego; second, the displacement of filial attachment onto a father substitute.

The Prince, in his thoughts, compares the King, his father, with an ideal of royal dignity far superior to the father himself. This ideal, derived from paternal figures but exalted and heightened, is his protection in the struggle against his parricidal impulses and against submission to the King. This mechanism operates in some form or other in every boy's development at the time of the resolution of the oedipal conflict. During this process the superego requires part of its severity and some of its autonomy. . . .

Prince Hal uses not only his ideal of moral integrity as reproachful contrast against his father, but also his own playful depravity. The second mechanism of defense the Prince mobilizes is no less common than the first. He adopts an extrafamilial substitute who, true to a pattern frequently observed, is the antithesis of the father. Falstaff is closer to the Prince's heart than the King; he satisfies the libidinal demands in the father-son relation through his warmth and freedom. Yet the Prince proves superior to Falstaff in wit and royal reveling: he triumphs over both father and father substitute.[5] He is paramount in license as he will be paramount in royal dignity.

[5] The son's superiority over the father occurs also in other connections in the trilogy. Hotspur is superior to both Worcester and Northumberland and Aumerle is superior to his father, York, who first betrays King Richard before he betrays his own son.

Chronology of Important Dates

	Shakespeare	Other Events
1558		Accession of Queen Elizabeth.
1564	Birth of Shakespeare.	Birth of Marlowe.
1572		Birth of Jonson and Donne.
1576		The Theatre, the first permanent playhouse, built by James Burbage.
1582	Marriage to Anne Hathaway.	
1587		Kyd's *The Spanish Tragedy*; Marlowe's *Tamburlaine*, Part I.
1588		Defeat of the Spanish Armada.
1590–92	The three parts of *Henry VI*; *The Comedy of Errors*.	Spenser's *Faerie Queene*, Books I–III (1590). Marlowe's *Doctor Faustus* and *Edward II* (1592).
1593–95	*Venus and Adonis* and *The Rape of Lucrece*; *Titus Andronicus*; *The Taming of the Shrew*; *Richard III*; *The Two Gentlemen of Verona*; *Love's Labour's Lost*.	Death of Marlowe (1593). The Lord Chamberlain's company formed with Shakespeare a sharer (1594).
1595–97	*A Midsummer Night's Dream*; *Richard II*; *Romeo and Juliet*; *King John*; *The Merchant of Venice*.	Spenser's *Faerie Queene*, Books IV–VI (1596).
1597–98	*Henry IV*, Parts One and Two; *Much Ado About Nothing*.	Bacon's *Essays* (1597).

1599–1600	*Henry V; Julius Caesar; As You Like It; Twelfth Night.*	Globe Theatre built. Death of Spenser (1599).
1600–3	*Hamlet; The Merry Wives of Windsor; All's Well That Ends Well; Troilus and Cressida.*	Death of Queen Elizabeth; accession of King James (1603).
1603–5	*Measure for Measure; Othello.*	The Lord Chamberlain's company now the King's Men (1603).
1605–6	*King Lear; Macbeth.*	Jonson's *Volpone* (1606).
1606–8	*Antony and Cleopatra; Coriolanus; Timon of Athens.*	
1608–13	Publication of the Sonnets; *Pericles; Cymbeline; The Winter's Tale; The Tempest; Henry VIII.* Shakespeare retires to Stratford.	The Blackfriar's Playhouse acquired by the King's Men (1609). Jonson's *The Alchemist* (1610). The King James Bible (1611).
1616	Death of Shakespeare.	
1620		Pilgrims land at Plymouth Rock.
1623	The First Folio edition of Shakespeare's plays.	
1625		Death of James I and accession of Charles I.

Notes on the Editor and Contributors

R. J. Dorius, the editor of this volume, is Visiting Professor of English at Wellesley College. He has published articles on Shakespeare's histories and edited *Henry V* for "The Yale Shakespeare."

C. L. Barber, Professor of English at the New York State University at Buffalo, is the author of *Shakespeare's Festive Comedy* and other studies of Shakespeare, Marlowe, and Milton.

Jonas A. Barish, Professor of English at the University of California, Berkeley, has written widely on Shakespeare, Jonson, and problems of drama.

A. C. Bradley (1851–1935), Professor of Poetry at Oxford, published *Shakespearean Tragedy* in 1904 and the *Oxford Lectures on Poetry* five years later.

John F. Danby, Professor of English Language and Literature at the University of North Wales in Bangor, is the author of *Shakespeare's Doctrine of Nature*.

William Empson, Professor of English at the University of Sheffield, is a poet and author of *Seven Types of Ambiguity, Some Versions of Pastoral, The Structure of Complex Words,* and many essays.

Northrop Frye, Professor at Victoria College, the University of Toronto, is the author of *Anatomy of Criticism, A Natural Perspective, Fools of Time,* and other works.

Eric La Guardia, Associate Professor of English at the University of Washington, is the author of *Nature Redeemed*.

A. R. Humphreys, Professor of English at the University of Leicester, is editor of *Henry IV,* Parts I and II, in the new "Arden Shakespeare," the best edited recent edition of the plays.

Harold Jenkins, Regius Professor of Rhetoric and English Literature at the University of Edinburgh, is General Editor of the "Arden Shakespeare" and the author of books on Chettle and Benlowes.

ERNST KRIS (1900–1957), a leading psychoanalyst and aesthetician, wrote *Psychoanalytic Explorations in Art.*

ROBERT LANGBAUM, Professor of English at the University of Virginia, is the author of *The Poetry of Experience: the Dramatic Monologue in Modern Literary Tradition.*

NORMAN RABKIN, Professor of English at the University of California, Berkeley, has published collections of essays on Shakespeare and Elizabethan drama.

HAROLD E. TOLIVER, Professor of English at the Irvine campus of the University of California, has published a study of Andrew Marvell and articles on Henryson and Dekker.

DEREK TRAVERSI, who has worked through the British Council and British Institute in various countries, is the author of *An Approach to Shakespeare* and other books on groups of Shakespeare's plays.

Selected Bibliography

Brooks, Cleanth, and Heilman, R. B. *Understanding Drama*. New York: Henry Holt, 1945. A useful discussion of the balance and unity of the play.

Dickinson, Hugh. "The Reformation of Prince Hal." *Shakespeare Quarterly*, XII (1961), 33–46. A carefully reasoned essay on Hal's redeeming of time.

Goddard, Harold C. *The Meaning of Shakespeare*. Chicago: The Chicago University Press, 1951. Measures Hal against Shakespeare's other protagonists and finds him wanting.

Granville-Barker, Harley. "From *Henry V* to *Hamlet*." In *Studies in Shakespeare*. Edited by Peter Alexander. London: Oxford University Press, 1964. A revision of an earlier essay; illuminating on Shakespeare's movement from the histories to the tragedies.

Jenkins, Harold. "Shakespeare's History Plays: 1900–1951." *Shakespeare Survey*, VI (1953), 1–15. Cambridge: The Cambridge University Press. A survey of scholarship.

Knoepflmacher, U. C. "The Humors as Symbolic Nucleus in *Henry IV, Part I*." *College English*, XXIV (1963), 497–501. The four humors, fragmented in the other characters, are balanced in Hal.

Reese, M. M. *The Cease of Majesty*. London: Edward Arnold, Inc., 1961. An overall view of the histories, with an emphasis upon the need for stability.

Ribner, Irving. *The English History Play in the Age of Shakespeare*. Princeton, N.J.: The Princeton University Press, 1957; revised 1965. Useful on the political and historical background; an extensive bibliography.

Richmond, H. M. *Shakespeare's Political Plays*. New York: Random House, 1967. A good statement concerning Hal's growth in maturity.

Rossiter, A. P. "Ambivalence: The Dialectic of the Histories." In *Angel with Horns*. Edited by Graham Storey, pp. 40–64. London: Longmans,

Green & Co., Ltd., 1961. One of the most suggestive single essays on the histories in relation to the tragedies.

Shaaber, M. A. "The Unity of *Henry IV.*" *Joseph Quincy Adams Memorial Studies,* pp. 217–27. Washington: The Folger Shakespeare Library, 1948. Part II was composed only after the success of Part I.

Stewart, J. I. M. "The Birth and Death of Falstaff." *Character and Motive in Shakespeare,* pp. 111–44. London: Longmans, Green & Co., Ltd., 1949. A helpful survey of conflicting interpretations and the development of a position similar to Barber's.

Stoll, E. E. *Shakespeare and Other Masters.* Cambridge, Mass.: Harvard University Press; London: Oxford University Press, 1940.

——. *Shakespeare Studies: Historical and Comparative in Method,* pp. 415–24. New York: The Macmillan Co., 1927. Sustained warfare against Bradley's emphasis upon character; theatrical conventions of the Renaissance.

Tillyard, E. M. W. *Shakespeare's History Plays.* London: Chatto & Windus, 1944; New York: The Macmillan Co., 1946. Relates the plays to an Elizabethan moral and political background deriving from the chroniclers.

Traversi, Derek. *Shakespeare from Richard II to Henry V.* Stanford, Calif.: Stanford University Press, 1957; London: Hollis & Carter, 1958. Detailed studies of poetic texture; Hal chiefly seen as a politician.

Wilson, J. Dover, ed. *Henry IV, Part I.* Cambridge: Cambridge University Press, 1946. A helpful and thorough critical edition.

——. *The Fortunes of Falstaff.* London: The Cambridge University Press, 1943; New York: The Macmillan Co., 1944. The liveliest of the studies relating the play to a prevailing morality pattern.

——, and Worsley, T. C. *Shakespeare's Histories at Stratford, 1951. New* York: Theatre Arts Books, 1952. Instructive account of the staging of the Lancastrian tetralogy.

For further helpful bibliographical leads, the student should consult the opening footnotes for the selections by Toliver and British in this collection.